Laurence Picamoles

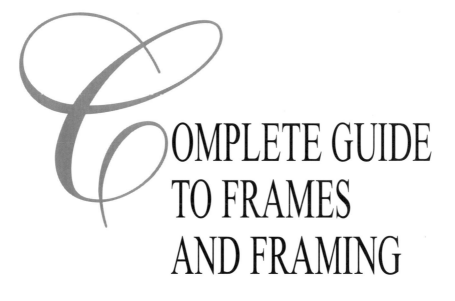

COMPLETE GUIDE TO FRAMES AND FRAMING

Photographs
Laurent Bianquis and Sylvie Vernichon

Illustrations
Ferdinand Doskha

HACHETTE
Illustrated

CONTENTS

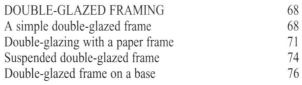

INTRODUCTION

A picture frame is not just for showing off an old master or other major work of art. These days it's possible to use a huge range of frames, classic or contemporary, to display family photographs, engravings, children's drawings, cartoon characters, floral compositions, all kinds of montages and collages, and even small objects and models, if their size allows. In short, a frame will highlight the originality of a creation.

Picture framing is a hobby that anyone can enjoy. It can be a leisure activity that fulfils the need to be creative and make something beautiful. It also satisfies the urge to do something practical with your hands. If you are at home with young children, for example, it is a craft that you can practise at the kitchen table, to create objects that give a personal touch to the decoration of your children's rooms. It allows you to give free rein to your imagination and reveal your hidden talents. As long as you follow a few basic rules, you will find that a huge range of effects is possible.

The choice of mouldings for frames is enormous, and ranges from classical styles in gilded wood, to informal natural pine, to elaborate designs encrusted with pearls or decorated with stencilled shells. The same goes for the mount medium and colour: you can choose from a range of plain, neutral-coloured surrounds for your picture, or make a more colourful one from canvas, denim or gingham. The choice is endless – the field of creativity knows no bounds.

Family photos and other memorabilia will have more impact if their
frames are striking and go with the décor of the room in which
they are displayed. A frame enhances an image; for example,
it can give new life to a monochrome engraving that might
otherwise be a little dull, enabling it to give us real pleasure
and find its true place in our living room. A bevelled edge can add
depth, and a well-chosen mount can also bring out a colour or
illuminate its subject. Indeed, a mixed-medium frame is the perfect
way to create a balanced ensemble and to show off a new-found
treasure, even one that might have seemed quite ordinary at first.

Since this is a hobby that does not require any special skills,
you can make your first frame for a picture whenever you choose.
However, it is essential to take your time, to be careful and painstaking.
Picture framing requires you to be accurate, especially when taking
measurements, cutting frames and preparing mounts. It would be
disappointing to find that you have cut a length of frame too short just
because you took one wrong measurement. This can be summed up in
the adage 'measure twice, cut once!' Carelessness can mean having to
start again from the beginning, although this is not the end of the world
because at least you won't spoil the subject you are framing.

This book is intended to help everyone successfully frame all
kinds of pictures in a variety of designs. It guides you step by step
through the making of various styles of frame. For every project,
a list of the materials you will need is followed by a clear
explanation of all the different stages of the work. It is important to
follow the instructions exactly to obtain perfect results. Helpful tips
throughout each section provide you with advice on making
the work easier, or ideas that will give your projects extra flair and
originality. Ultimately, the satisfaction of creating personalised frames
means that, once you have mastered the basic techniques, you will
want to give free rein to your creativity and adapt the ideas in this book
to suit your own interiors and colour schemes.

TOOLS AND MATERIALS

You don't need much space for picture framing, but it is essential that your work surface is completely stable. A kitchen or dining table is suitable, as long as you protect it from scratches from your cutter with two layers of thick card. Alternatively, use a sheet of fibreboard supported on two trestles.

Materials

For your first framing project you can use basic everyday tools, although for a full range of equipment you will need some items from specialist suppliers.

Plastic paper knife
Compass with pencil tip
Small hammer with heavy head
Pin hammer
Heavy metal ruler for cutting card
Cutter with angled tip
Large box of trapezoid blades for the cutter
Plastic 45° set square
Nail punch, size 1 or 2
20-in (50-cm) metal scale ruler
Box of ½, ¾ and 1-in (12, 15 and 25-mm) nails
Box of 1½-in (3-cm) pins
Small universal pliers
Cutting pliers
Two pasting brushes of different widths
Pair of pointed scissors
No. 8 and no. 14 paintbrushes
Strong brown adhesive tape

Bradawl
Two small 1-lb (½-kg) weights. You may use any weights, provided they are flat-bottomed and clean
Cord clamp for assembling mouldings; the angles holding each corner are held together by nylon cord twisted taut
Two rolls of brown gummed paper tape; one 1 in (2.5 cm) wide (to stick the subject to the mounting card and to seal the back of a small frame) and the other 1¾ in (4.5 cm) wide (to seal the back of a larger frame)
Bevelling ruler. This is a metal scale ruler fitted with a cutter at a 45° angle. It is quite expensive, but does make bevelling easier.
Four clamps

1 Glasspaper
2 Cord clamp
3 Cutter
4 Dry-point
5 Metal rings
6 Screw eyes
7 Universal pliers
8 Hammer
9 Cutter blades
10 Nail punch
11 Metal scale ruler
12 Heavy metal ruler
13 Paper knife
14 Metal fasteners and
hanging rings
15 Set square
16 Cord
17 Paintbrushes
18 Pasting brushes
19 Brass nails
20 Pins
21 Ruler and cutter
for bevelled edges
22 Felt-tip pen
23 Pencil
24 Brown gummed
paper tape,
1¾in (4.5 cm)
25 Brown gummed
paper tape,
1 in (2.5 cm)
26 Strong brown
adhesive tape
27 Scissors
28 Neoprene glue
29 Mitre box
30 Screwdriver
31 Bradawl
32 Clear satin varnish
33 PVA adhesive
34 Mitre saw
35 Hinges
36 Wood glue

Large tools

The mitre box and saw

A mitre box enables you to start cutting mouldings using a simple wood saw, but you may find that the blade of such a saw soon wears out and that the teeth become twisted out of shape. This will mean that you cannot cut mouldings accurately, making it difficult to assemble them properly. It is then best to change to a proper mitre saw. Mitre saws are available in three sizes. A medium-sized one is the most useful, since it will be stable enough to cut thick, heavy mouldings, and also suitable for smaller ones.

If you are not thoroughly familiar with forming mitred corners using a mitre box, carry out a couple of trial runs before starting on an actual frame moulding. Since the mitre box must not move while you are cutting, screw the base of the box to the centre of a piece of fibreboard about 3 ft (1 m) long and 8 in (20 cm) wide, using two screws. Fix the board to the work surface with two clamps.

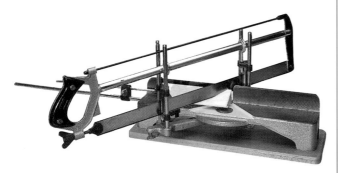

Frame saw

The frame saw

A frame saw is expensive, but is the best type to use if you are going to do a lot of framing. It has a stop that enables you to cut any number of mouldings to a pre-determined size – you only need to take one measurement. It is also very accurate.

Backing board, mountboard, card and paper

Grey card
Use this card to protect your work surface. On average, each piece will measure 32 × 48 in (80 × 120 cm). You need to use two thicknesses, as your cutter may penetrate the top layer.

Wood pulp board
This board, made of compressed paper pulp, comes in various thicknesses, in sheets measuring 32 × 48 in (80 × 120 cm). There are three types:
• Backing board
This is the first element to prepare, whatever type of frame you choose. It is stiff, beige-coloured card, to which you can fix hanging attachments.
It is usually $\frac{1}{12}$ in (2 mm) thick and weighs 48 oz/sq yd (1,500 g/m²).
• Mountboard
This is thick card for making mounts that will form a border and give depth or relief to a picture.
It is $\frac{1}{10}$ in (3 mm) thick, weighs 58 oz/sq yd (1,800 g/m²), and comes in various colours.
• Bevelling board
This is extra thick mountboard used for making deeply bevelled mounts.

Mounting or backing card
This is a thinner type of card, which you can also use to make mounts that you then cover with decorative paper, fabric, paint or pigments. You can also use it as an extra layer between subject and backing board, to even out irregularities caused by attachments.

1 Canson, Ingres and Bristol paper in a variety of colours
2 Fabric papers in a variety of colours
3 Bookbinding papers, papyrus, imitation lizard skin, embossed, marbled and manila papers in a variety of colours

Tip

For larger pictures, up to
32 × 48 in (80 × 120 cm),
use $\frac{1}{10}$-in (3-mm) thick board
as the backing board. For subjects larger
than this, use hardboard or fibreboard.

Decorative card and paper

Decorative card consists of a layer of Canson, Ingres or laid paper glued to thick card. It comes in various colours, and is used for making mounts. This is an alternative to making your own mount, whether bevelled or not, by covering mounting card or mountboard with decorative paper yourself. Decorative papers include bookbinding paper, brown paper, imitation leather paper, lizardskin paper and marbled paper.

Tip

You could also use wallpaper offcuts to cover a mount.

Fabrics

You can save fabric offcuts for covering mounts. There are no rules for choosing fabrics, but make sure that they are thick enough to ensure that glue does not show through.

Glues

PVA adhesive

This is used for gluing card and pieces of fabric and paper. When covering, ensure that no glue spills on to the work surface because it may stain.

Wood glue

This is used for gluing wood, when assembling the frame mouldings.

Neoprene glue

This is for gluing balsa mouldings at the back of double-glazed framed subjects and when framing mirrors. It forms a bond very quickly.

Glass

The most suitable glass for the majority of picture framing projects is $\frac{1}{12}$ in (2 mm) thick. However, for large items it is better to use $\frac{1}{10}$-in (3-mm) thick glass, as thinner glass would be too fragile and easily broken. Non-reflective glass or Perspex may also be used. Perspex is more expensive than glass, but it is light and so can be useful for very large frames, which are heavy in themselves.

Cutting glass to size

It is useful to know how to cut glass to size so that you can make your own made-to-measure pieces. This requires a certain amount of practice, especially in the case of double-glazed frames (see pages 68–77), when all your cuts need to be absolutely straight. If you are not sure of yourself, it is better to consult a glazier.

If you want to cut the glass yourself, buy sheets of glass that are not too big, and no thicker than $\frac{1}{12}$ to $\frac{1}{10}$ in (2 to 3 mm). If you need thicker glass (or you are not sure of your cutting ability), it's better to have it cut by a specialist.

Materials

Heavy ruler – Marker pen
Thick felt – Glass cutter
Household glove – Oil in a glass container

Method

1 *Cover your work surface with thick felt or a tablecloth, making sure that it is smooth.*

2 *Place the glass on it, and check that the bottom left-hand corner is truly square.*

Transfer the measurements of the backing board to the glass. With a felt-tip pen join the two points, and then draw a second parallel line 1/12 to 1/10 in (2 to 3 mm) to the left of the first. This corresponds to the thickness of the glass cutter and ensures that the glass will be cut to precisely the right measurements.

4 *Slide the piece of glass to be cut off to the edge of the work-table. Hold the piece to be used for the frame flat on the table, pressing it down with your left hand. Grip the part to be removed with your right hand and snap downwards. It should come off in a single piece.*

5 *Repeat the procedure to cut the other side of the glass to size.*

Tip

If the part to be removed does not snap off in one piece, very gently tap beneath the full length of the score with the glass cutter to deepen the cut. You may also use pliers.

3 *Place the heavy ruler on this second line. Dip the glass cutter in the oil and position it on top of the glass, pressing it against the ruler but keeping it vertical over the surface of the glass. Score the glass by running the cutter down the line, to the bottom edge of the glass.*

Tip

Always dip the glass cutter in oil before each use.
Before lifting up the cut piece of glass, put on a glove to avoid cutting your hand.

Mouldings

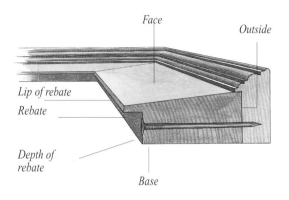

Face
Outside
Lip of rebate
Rebate
Depth of rebate
Base

A picture frame is made up of four pieces of moulding fitted together at the corners, which have been cut to shape at 45°. Before embarking on the task of putting a frame together, it's important to know the precise terms for each part of the moulding, as shown in the drawing above. Frame moulding pieces generally come in lengths of 6 ft 6 in or 9 ft 9 in (2 or 3 m).

1 Backing board
2 Mountboard
3 Mounting card
4 and 5 Beige and red micro-corrugated paper
6 Multiple photo-frame-type mount
7 Yellow Bristol paper
8 Rustic-style natural wood moulding painted red
9 Natural wood mouldings in various widths
10 Balsa moulding
11 Carved moulding with white finish
12 Renaissance-style moulding with painted marquetry
13 Cherry veneer moulding with gilded inner edge

14 Period gilded rebate with ornate inner edge
15 Ornamental moulding with antique gilded paint
16 Dark grey bamboo-style moulding
17 Mahogany veneer moulding with black fillets
18 Classical-style black moulding
19 Classical-style natural wood moulding with beaded fillet
20 Classical-style moulding in natural wood, varnished
21 Blue needlecord moulding

Size

For smaller frames, use a narrow moulding with a face (top surface) about ½ to ⅞ in (1 to 2 cm) wide. For larger frames, use wider mouldings measuring about 1⅛ to 2½ in (3 to 6 cm) wide.

Tip

For an original effect, you can use a wide moulding to make a tiny frame.

Form and style

There are many different kinds of moulding: natural or gilded wood, flat or rounded, pointed or concave. If your home is decorated in the Regency, Victorian or Edwardian style, you can choose mouldings to match, and these are generally gilded or in dark wood.

Colour

Simple mouldings in natural wood may be left as they are or painted in one of the dominant colours of the picture being framed. Once you have decided on the colour, use a special wood paint or acrylic paint. Of course, wooden mouldings are also available already finished, either painted, lacquered or varnished, limed or with marquetry or other detailing.

Measurements

The dimensions of the moulding depend on the size of the backing board, whatever style of frame you choose.

Once you have chosen the moulding, carry out the following calculations to find out the total length of moulding needed. For example, for a backing board measuring 8 × 6 in (20 × 15 cm), add these measurements together and multiply by two (8 + 6 = 14 in; 14 × 2 = 28 in (20 + 15 = 35 cm; 35 × 2 = 70 cm)). Measure the width of the face of the moulding (e.g. 1 in (2.5 cm) wide) and multiply by eight (1 × 8 = 8 (2.5 × 8 = 20 cm)), because when the moulding is cut there will be eight offcuts. Add this 8-in (20-cm) offcut allowance to the 28 in (70 cm) to give a total of 36 in (90 cm). Always allow an additional margin of 4 in (10 cm). The length of moulding needed for a backing board of 8 × 6 in (20 × 15 cm) is therefore 40 in (100 cm).

In order to check that the diagonal cuts in the moulding are identical and fit together well, lay them flat and position the corners against one another.

Tip

In a specialist shop it's possible to have mouldings cut when you buy them. Don't forget the measurements of your backing board when buying a length of moulding.

Attachments

The hanging attachment that is easiest to fix and most frequently used is a small metal ring with a metal lug, which is attached to the backing board. Larger or heavier frames should be hung on the wall by cord or picture wire, threaded between two metal screw eyes that are fixed to each side of the frame at the back.

Tip

If possible, always fix hanging attachments to the backing rather than the frame, because attachments nailed or screwed to the frame may be partly visible, especially if the moulding is narrow.

THE LANGUAGE OF COLOUR

When we talk about colours being harmonious we are making a judgement about the effects of juxtaposing certain colours. Although people will often have different opinions about whether particular colours go together (according to their habits, impressions and personal taste), certain criteria, such as balance, strength and symmetry, may be considered objectively. In order fully to appreciate a particular colour it is best to place it against a neutral grey background.

Scientific studies of colour theory show that there are seven basic shades, which can be obtained by splitting white light with a prism. The full spectrum is covered by what are known as the three primary colours: yellow, red and blue. Traditionally, painters have used yellows to lighten and blues to add shadow to their work, but adding white or black also influences the luminosity and the saturation of all colours. Dilution with water or solvent also changes the nature of colours: the opaque shades of undiluted paint become more transparent when diluted.

The colour palette

Using a colour wheel is helpful when choosing colours, and when mixing your own. The example here is divided into 12 sections, and is based on the three primary colours, yellow, red and blue. It is important to choose these carefully when buying paints.

Start by drawing an equilateral triangle. Place yellow in the top part of the triangle, blue at bottom left, and red at bottom right. Draw a circle around this triangle and then insert a hexagon between the circle and the triangle, thus obtaining three additional triangles. Fill in these triangles with the colours obtained by mixing the three primary colours, to create the three secondary colours, as follows:

blue + red = violet; yellow + red = orange; yellow + blue = green.

To obtain 'true' secondary colours, the primary colours must be mixed exactly half and half. Violet should be neither too blue nor too red, green should be neither too yellow nor too blue, and so on.

Draw a second circle with a reasonable spacing outside the first, forming a ring. Divide this ring

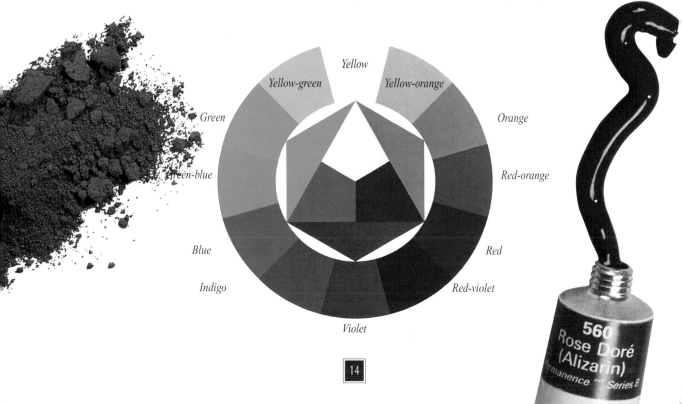

Yellow
Yellow-green
Yellow-orange
Green
Orange
Green-blue
Red-orange
Blue
Red
Indigo
Red-violet
Violet

560 Rose Doré (Alizarin) Permanence ··· Series B

Mixing colours

Here are two methods for creating a range of mixed colours.

1. Colour triangle
Mark each side of an equilateral triangle into three equal sections. Join up these points in pairs, forming two lines parallel to each side of the triangle, giving you nine new equal-sized triangles. Fill the three angles with yellow, red and blue, and then fill the middle triangles in between with yellow and red, yellow and blue, and red and blue. Each of the remaining triangles should be filled in with the colour obtained from mixing the three surrounding colours. You can also make up a colour triangle starting with different colours from those used in this example.

2. Colour strips
Draw quite a wide strip on a piece of drawing paper. At each end place a colour of your choice, then mix them progressively. The intervening shades produced may be lightened or darkened. As with the colour triangle, you can do this using any combination of colours.

into 12 equal sections. Next, fill in these sections in order, leaving a blank space between each colour. These empty spaces will be filled with the six tertiary colours, obtained by mixing a primary colour with a secondary colour, as follows:

blue + violet =indigo;

blue + green = green-blue;

yellow + green = yellow-green;

yellow + orange = yellow-orange;

red + orange = red-orange;

red + violet = red-violet.

The colours appear in the same order as a rainbow or a projection through a prism.

Among these shades, some have a warming, or 'tonic' feel, and are known as warm or hot colours. This group includes yellow, yellow-orange, red-orange, red and red-violet. By comparison, certain colours appear to recede or be deeper, and are known as cool or cold colours: yellow-green, green, green-blue, blue, indigo and violet.

Of course these distinctions are relative, but they may help you when choosing.

Although you can buy many different shades of blue, red, yellow, green, and so on, it is just as easy to make up your own colours based on the primary colours, plus black and white. Make up a trial palette on piece of paper, writing down the make-up of each shade, so that you can reproduce it easily whenever you need it.

Choosing colours

Colour communicates mood. For example, pale, neutral or natural colours are calmer than bright ones. The impact of a colour is also influenced by the colours adjacent to it.

Yellow is the brightest colour and has a radiant, enlivening effect when contrasted with more sombre tones. Its brightness decreases against a pink background, and increases against a green background. It is luminous against blue, and appears stronger when contrasted with a white background.

Red is a hot colour with a strong luminosity that is difficult to tone down. It is particularly striking when it has a yellowish or bluish hue. Against an orange background it will look more sombre, while a black background will give it a demonic, dangerous quality.

Blue is always a cool colour. Against a light violet background it will seem dull, and it will transform brown into a bright colour. Against a red-orange background blue will seem darker, stronger and brighter. Manganese oxide blue mixed with yellow gives a particularly bright tone of green.

Before deciding on the colours to use for your frame and mount, it is important to consider all the colours in the subject you are framing.

Powder pigments

You can use these powders as they are, to give a simple finish to wooden mouldings (see page 17) and mounts of every type. They can also be mixed with water and used like watercolours, for washes on mounts in the same way as coloured inks (see below), and to create a variety of different effects.

Wood paints and textured paints

These may be used to colour wooden mouldings and bevelled edges. They are available from picture framers, artists' suppliers and some larger stores. They come in all the essential colours (white, green, red, yellow and blue), which can be mixed to give other shades.

Watercolours

Since these are quite expensive, you can start by building up a palette of essential colours. These are permanent yellow, Indian yellow, cobalt green, rose doré and cerulean blue, which will provide a good basis from which to create other colours. Watercolour can be used on mounts, as a wash or to add decorative details.

Inks

You can use inks for line and wash borders (see page 92), and for other decorative effects. Rotring inks (used by architects) are the best for all-round use. Brown and black are the colours to use for drawing fine lines, or fillets, round a mount. For washes, choose inks in other colours, which you dilute with water.

TECHNIQUES FOR DECORATING WOOD

Simple finishes

There are several techniques for finishing and giving a feeling of age to new wooden mouldings. You can achieve a lovely sheen by simply waxing surfaces, or colour beeswax with oil paints or pigments before applying it. Translucent varnish gives an excellent finish, but may not set very hard, and will need a protective coat of wax. Patina wood finish will set harder.

For a more opaque, velvety finish, rub on some powder pigment with cotton wool, or dab painted surfaces with a light wash of watered-down emulsion paint, or satin lacquer diluted with white spirit. Apply the paint or lacquer with a cloth or brush, depending on the desired effect.

Gesso, available in pots from specialist picture framers or fine arts retailers, and generally used to coat canvases, can also be used to decorate mouldings. Either brush it on or use it to form relief motifs. Before it dries, you can add special effects with a comb, toothbrush, cloth, your fingers or by adding pigments. If you want a smooth surface, simply allow the gesso to dry thoroughly before giving it a light sanding with fine glasspaper. It can then be finished with inks, pigments or diluted paint.

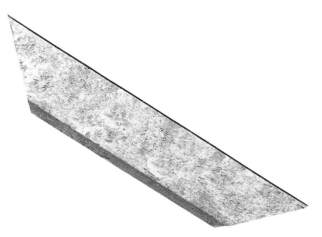

Ageing painted wood

This technique has the advantage of being suitable for old as well as new wood. Prepare old wood that has already been treated, such as old frame mouldings or plinths (used to make certain types of frame), by sanding it thoroughly with coarse

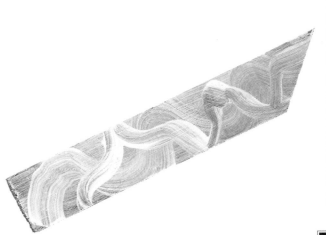

and then fine glasspaper. Choose water-based emulsion rather than oil-based paint, or gesso mixed with pigments. Don't worry if the wood fibres swell up from the effect of the water, as you will be sanding them down. This technique gives wood a rough, faded, distressed appearance. Protect the finish with matt, satin or gloss varnish, depending on the effect you require.

Crackle glazes

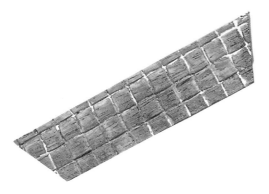

Newly painted mouldings may be given added effect with a crackle glaze. Decorative crackle glazes on porcelain and pottery first appeared in Europe in the 18th century, inspired by oriental china and some Japanese ceramics.

The procedure is simple. It involves applying two different varnishes, which react with one another to give a crackle glaze. The first is a flexible, oil-based varnish that dries slowly and the second is a water-based varnish that dries quickly. You apply the second layer of varnish while the first is still slightly tacky. The crackled effect produced by the reaction between the two kinds of varnish won't show until dust settles in the fine cracks. Alternatively, you can rub thick oil-based paint over the moulding, to penetrate the cracks and highlight them. Don't use this kind of colouring with deep reliefs, however, because it won't dry properly if the cracks in the glaze run too deep.

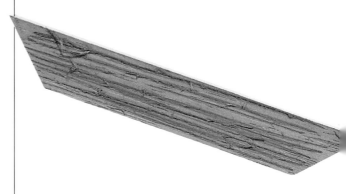

Another way of colouring the cracks is to use thick transparent varnish mixed with oil-based earthy colours (one part varnish, one part colour) such as terre-verte (greyish-green) or raw umber (greenish-brown). To emphasise further the patina of a crackle glaze finish, and for a beautiful and original effect, use dilute ink on a toothbrush to add small patches of colour here and there.

STRETCHING A PICTURE

If the subject to be framed is slightly warped or creased, it cannot always be straightened out fully under a press. To eliminate these faults, use the following procedure.

Materials

Piece of glass bigger than the subject
Sponge and a saucer of water – Brown gummed paper tape

1 *Lay your piece of glass flat and clean the surface thoroughly.*

2 *Cut two strips of brown gummed tape longer than the width of the picture. These are to hold it in place.*

3 *Place the picture face down on the glass. Hold it down and use a damp sponge, squeezed out, to wipe it from top to bottom over the whole surface.*

4 *Place the sponge in the saucer of water. Hold one of the strips of tape flat, the adhesive side against the sponge. Pressing the tape down with one hand, draw it through with the other hand, moistening it all along its length.*

5 *Position the tape along one long edge of the picture, no more than ½ in (1 cm) in, so that it overlaps the edge. Stick it down on to the glass, smoothing it down quickly with the palm of your hand.*

Tip

Ensure that the tape is not creased when it is stuck down, as this could cause additional creases in the picture.

6 *Pass the sponge, barely damp this time, once more very lightly over the picture to stretch it, and then stick the other piece of tape along the opposite side in the same way as before.*

7 *Leave it to dry. When the item is well stretched, you can remove the strips of tape. To do this, moisten them slightly with the sponge before pulling them off gently. Don't try to remove any small bits of brown paper that may remain, since this might permanently damage your picture.*

HANGING PICTURES

There are many ways of hanging framed pictures. You can use simple nails, or single- or double-pin picture hooks, with a single metal ring on the back of a picture or, for bigger pictures, screw eyes and picture wire. A more elaborate arrangement is to make the hanging visible, using wide or narrow ribbon or haberdashery cord, and this offers an additional way of personalising the decoration of a room.

Given that a picture will be a focal point once it is on the wall, the way in which it is hung deserves careful attention. The picture will only be displayed at its best if hung in the right place. In order to do this, you need to consider various factors, such as the available space, the number of pictures to be hung and the style and lighting of the room.

You can choose to group pictures according to their style or subject matter, type of frame, or because their colours go together. Alternatively, you might wish to highlight a single work by hanging it alone. Frames may be hung symmetrically or more informally. However, it is best not to hang a collection of pictures completely at random. To visualise how a composition of several pictures will look on the wall, arrange them on the floor first.

Keep a certain amount of space between each picture, aligning them either by the edge of their frames or by the edge of the image. You can hang them vertically or horizontally. In all cases, make good use of different alignments. It is better not to position original framed pictures side by side.

In a living room or dining room, don't hang a picture too high in relation to your eye level when sitting, or its proportions will be visually distorted. On the other hand, you can hang pictures higher up the wall in corridors, entrance halls, bedrooms, kitchens and bathrooms.

Don't hang pictures in direct sunlight, since this could fade and spoil the colours. It could also cause unwanted reflections from the glass of a picture.

Get another person to help you when you are actually hanging pictures on the wall. This will not only help you make sure that they are aligned and in balance, but will also give you a second opinion about the final position of a picture before you fix it in place.

Various different ways of arranging pictures are described below.

Grid pattern

This requires several smallish pictures, six or more, all the same size and evenly spaced in rows. The lateral spaces should be slightly narrower than the vertical spacing, in order to give a symmetrical effect to the grid.

Mosaic pattern

This composition requires pictures of different sizes and shapes. To create the right effect, put larger pictures on the outer edges of the arrangement, and smaller pictures in the spaces between them.

Rows

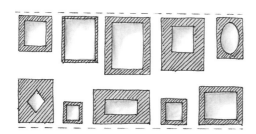

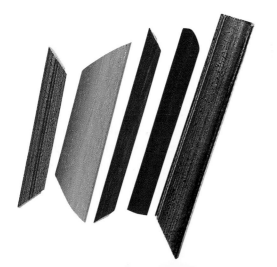

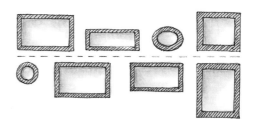

You can arrange pictures in rows in one of the following ways:
• aligned along their top edges;
• aligned along their bottom edges;
• aligned through their centres.
For an arrangement of two rows of pictures, you can align either the top or bottom row along their bottom edges, and the other row along their top edges.

Around a central point

Imagine a central point on the floor where a horizontal and a vertical axis intersect. Align your pictures around this imaginary cross, with the larger ones positioned towards the middle of the arrangement. This will give a balanced effect that still allows for an asymmetrical look. Choose the area of wall where you wish to place the collection, and fix the items in position.

Using trimmings

A group of small pictures in a similar style may be hung from ribbon. One way of doing this is to thread a length of ribbon through the hanging ring at the back of each picture and make a bow to lie at the top of the frame. You could also tie a bow about 6 in (15 cm) above the frame, allowing the ends of the ribbon to hang down the wall. In this case the picture will hang from this point and jut out slightly. Cut off the ends of the ribbon at an angle.

• Fishing wire is very strong and can be used to hang a large, heavy picture. As this wire is practically invisible it will create a spectacular effect. To do this, fix a double picture hook at the top of the wall, close to the ceiling. Let the fishing wire hang down to the required height and fix it to the attachments at the back of the picture.

• Using haberdashery cord can give the impression that several pictures are attached to each other. Knots, bows and little circles can be created in the spaces between them. The ensemble effect gives an added touch of originality to the decoration of a room.

Again, it is advisable to try out the arrangement of pictures and cords on the floor first, in order to get the spatial proportions right.

Using a ruler, determine the spacing between each picture and that between the swags, knots and bows. Transfer these to the wall using a pencil, lightly marking the position of each element before fixing them (the knots, swags, bows and pictures) in place.

Affix small nails where the pictures and knots or bows will be, to hold them in place on the wall. Position the pictures and then the trimmings, tying them to the picture attachments.

PICTURE FRAMING TECHNIQUES

This elementary technique is the first one to master. It applies to all the projects, since it shows you how to construct a basic frame into which you can place any kind of subject. Here we show you how to cut and assemble mouldings. It is important to prepare all your materials in advance, and to remember that care and precision are essential.

SIMPLE PICTURE FRAMING

MATERIALS

Moulding   Metal scale rule
Backing board   Hammer
Metal hanging ring   Cutter
1¾-in (4.5-cm)   Mitre box
brown gummed paper   Wood glue
tape   Emery board
Strong brown adhesive   Cloth
tape   Sponge
Cord clamp   Glass
Heavy ruler   ½-in (12-mm) pins

This framing method is an economical way of displaying and protecting a picture. In contrast to a simple clip frame, using your own choice of wooden moulding adds an effective touch. It can be left plain, or painted to suit the subject. This technique is particularly appropriate for children's drawings, posters, maps or shipping charts, large-format photos or reproductions of paintings or engravings. It adds style to the most standard subject.

Measuring and cutting the backing board

Before you start, make sure that you take precise measurements of the item to be framed and check that its sides and angles are perfectly square. If they are not, turn the picture face down and use a metal ruler and set square to square off the edges, drawing pencil lines to precise dimensions. Place a heavy ruler on these lines and cut the picture square with the cutter.

Tip
Don't cut your picture if it is valuable, but fold it with a paper knife to the size you require.

1 *Measure the width and height of the picture. Transfer these measurements to the backing board, using a pencil and metal scale rule.*

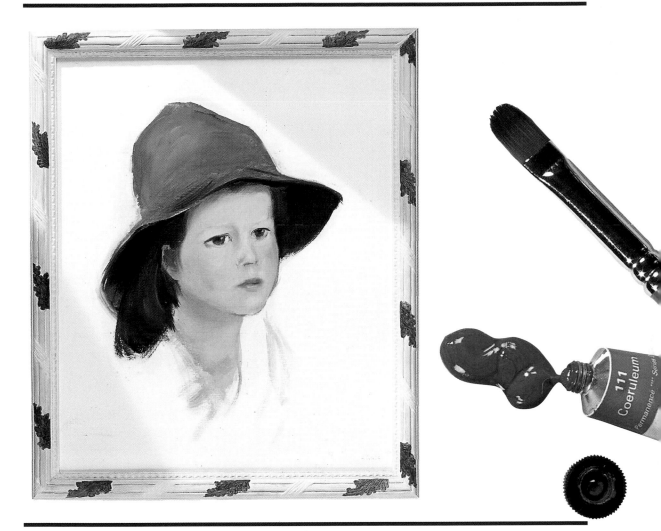

draw the cutter down along the ruler, keeping the point of the blade perpendicular to the board and cutting from top to bottom. As you cut, follow the line of the cut along the ruler with your other hand, maintaining strong, even pressure.
You may need to do this two or three times to cut right through the board.

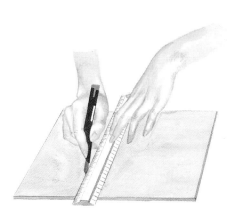

2 Cut the board along the pencil lines, using the cutter and the heavy ruler. Place the ruler between two points and check that it is precisely in position. Holding it steady with one hand,

Tip

Always position the cutter on the offcut side, so you don't spoil the work if it slips. It is helpful to mark a cross on what will be the bottom of the backing board.

Fixing the hanging attachment

1 Find the centre of the backing board by measuring, and mark it with a pencil. Mark a line one fifth to one quarter of the way down from the top of the board.

2 Make a longitudinal cut with the cutter, using strong pressure to ensure it goes right through the backing board.

3 Take the metal hanging ring. Slide the lugs through the slit. Turn the backing board over.

4 Cut down through the top layer of the board round the lugs, to create a hollow area, and remove this thin layer of card.

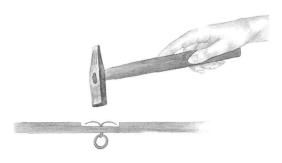

5 Flatten out the lugs of the ring attachment with a hammer, then hold them in place with a piece of adhesive tape.

Tip

For a larger picture, affix two rings. Make a mark about 4 in (10 cm) in from the edge of each side of the board, at the same height as for a single attachment. Thread a nylon cord through the two rings. If the framed picture is heavy, it's better to use screw eyes and picture wire as an attachment system.

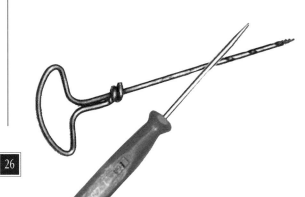

Measuring, cutting and assembling the moulding

To make your frame successfully, always follow two fundamental rules:
• measure the backing board precisely;
• cut the moulding precisely.

1 *Measure the length and width of the backing board. Add ¹⁄₁₀ in (3 mm) to these*

measurements (for example, 8 in (20 cm) long + ¹⁄₁₀ in (3 mm) = 8¹⁄₁₀ in (20.3 cm), and 6 in (15 cm) wide + ¹⁄₁₀ in (3 mm) = 6¹⁄₁₀ in (15.3 cm)).

2 *Subtract the width of the moulding rebate (¼ in (5 mm) in this example): 8¹⁄₁₀ in (20.3 cm) – ½ in (1 cm) (¼ in/5 mm × 2) and 6¹⁄₁₀ in (15.3 cm) – ½ in (1 cm) (¼ in/5 mm × 2), which gives 7³⁄₅ × 5³⁄₅ in (19.3 × 14.3 cm).*

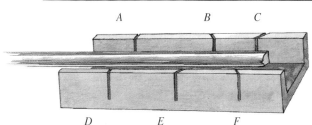

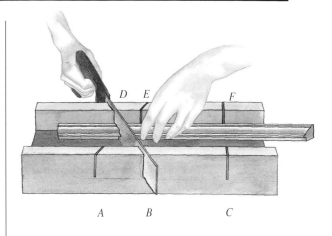

3 For the first angle, place the back of the moulding against side A, B, C of the mitre box. Slide it to just past the line of mitre grooves C and E.

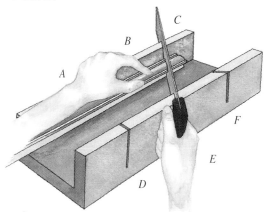

4 Place your index finger on top of the moulding, holding it with your thumb against the A, B, C side of the mitre box. Cut through C and E, and remove the moulding.

6 Place the back of the moulding against the D, E, F side of the mitre box, allowing the cut angle to extend beyond the left-hand outside edge. Precisely align the measured mark with the D to B intersection of the mitre box. Holding the moulding firmly against the D, E, F side of the mitre box so that it does not move, make the cut. Remove the cut portion of the moulding.

7 Proceed in the same way, repeating steps 3 to 6, to cut the other three sides of the frame to size.

8 Once the four sides have been cut to size, gently sand the eight angles with an emery board, to remove all splinters and irregularities. Do this carefully, to ensure that you don't distort the angles.

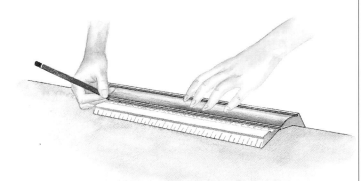

5 Position the moulding on the edge of the table, so that the width of the rebate rests against the surface of the table. Place the ruler against the lip of the moulding, with the scale starting at the first angle. Using a pencil, mark the length of the moulding (in this example, $7\frac{3}{5}$ in (19.3 cm)). This will give you the position of the second angle.

Tip

Remove any dust and splinters with your thumb, otherwise the adhesive will not take properly.

9 *Take the cord clamp and lay it on the work surface. Extend the cord so that there is enough room to insert the frame moulding pieces.*

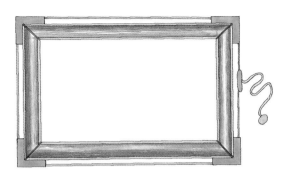

10 *Take one of the longer lengths of moulding and place it between the top two corner pieces of the clamp. Next, take a shorter length and place it between the top left and bottom left corner clamps. Continue with the remaining pieces. Once all pieces are in place, gently tighten the cord with your right hand to position the frame.*

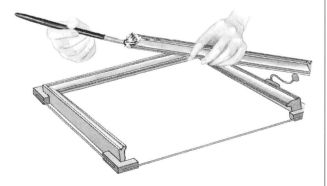

11 *Now slacken the clamp slightly so that you can take out the top length of moulding. Brush wood glue on to the two angles, and replace immediately in position within the clamp.*
Repeat for each of the other moulding pieces.

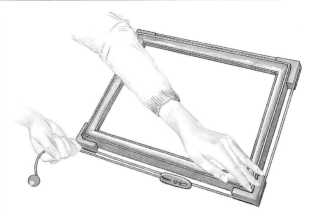

12 *Once you have applied the glue and replaced all the pieces in the cord clamp, press down diagonally on the frame with your left arm, your hand on the top right angle, and tighten the clamp cord with your right hand. Pull hard until it is fully tightened and lock in place with the fixing provided for the purpose. With a damp cloth, remove all surplus glue from the top of the moulding.*

13 *For a small frame, leave to set for three to four hours; allow six to eight hours for a larger frame. After this time, remove the cord clamp. Use a damp sponge and a cloth to remove all further glue residue from the corners of the frame. Smooth the corners with the emery board.*

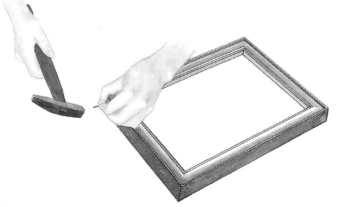

14 *Hammer a small pin into each corner from the side of the frame, taking care not to mark the moulding with the hammer. This holds the frame firmly in place.*

Final assembly

1 *In the following order, lay the backing board, the picture and the glass – spotlessly clean – on your work surface.*

2 *Place a weight on the glass and position the assembled pieces so that they slightly overlap the edge of the work surface.*

3 *Cut four pieces of brown gummed paper tape to the exact length of each side.*

4 *For correct positioning of the tape on the glass, mark a dotted line $\frac{1}{10}$ in (3 mm) from the edge of the tape.*

5 *Place the ruler along this dotted line. Using the paper knife, fold up this narrow edge strip. Make a sharp crease with the edge of the paper knife.*

6 *Moisten one of the strips of tape with a damp sponge. Place the narrow edge of the tape on the surface of the glass, and press down gently with the thumbs, starting from the middle and working out towards the ends.*

7 *Without moving the assembled pieces, smooth the tape over the side edge and then down on to the back of the backing board.*

8 *Turn this whole package through 90 degrees and repeat steps 6 and 7 to fix the tape along the other sides.*

Tip

If the adhesive tape is incorrectly positioned round the layers, remove it by moistening and rubbing. Check that the glass is clean again before refixing the tape.

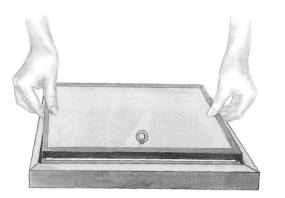

9 *Turn the frame face down on the work surface. Insert the package centrally within the frame. If necessary, wedge it by packing small pieces of card between the package and the frame in each corner. It is important that these wedges don't protrude above the rebate or the backing board.*

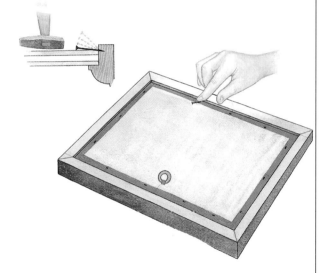

10 *Partially insert pins into the eight angles of the frame rebate, through and parallel to the backing board, keeping the pins in position with your index finger. Turn your framed picture over and check with the ruler that the picture is correctly centred. If not, remove the pins with pliers and reposition the package. Once it is properly centred, hammer the pins into the corners, and then add more at intervals along the four sides, through the backing board. The package must not move inside the frame.*

11 *To prevent dust and moisture from entering your frame, place strips of brown gummed paper tape over the gaps between the backing board and the back of the frame. Start with the longer sides. Measure one long side, placing the non-adhesive surface against the frame. Cut this length twice. In the same way, cut two lengths for the shorter sides.*

12 *Put a damp sponge in a saucer. Place the gummed side of one end of the tape against the sponge, keeping it flat with slight pressure from your hand, and draw the tape across the sponge to moisten it.*

13 *Stick the tape down, to the back of the moulding first and starting from the centre, smoothing it down over the join with your thumbs.*

14 *Repeat steps 12 and 13 for the three other sides.*

Mounts are positioned between the picture and the glass. In addition to their decorative function, this additional thickness creates a space between the two elements that promotes the passage of air and prevents condensation. The cut-away opening at the centre of the mount, which may take various forms depending on the required effect, is called the window.

$\mathcal{M}$OUNTS

MATERIALS

Mountboard	Frame
Scale rule	1¾-in (4.5-cm) brown
Heavy ruler	gummed paper tape
Cutter	½-in (12-mm) pins
Backing card	Damp sponge
Backing board	Glass
Brown gummed paper	Pencil
Paper knife	Fine glasspaper

FRAMING WITH A MOUNT

Mounts may be made of ready-finished mountboard, available in a variety of colours, or you can make your own decorative mount using backing or mounting card as a base. This card can be finished with a decorative paper, such as bookbinding paper, coloured papers or paper-backed tissue, or with pigments or paint.

Tip

It is easier to make your first mount using ready-finished mountboard.

Taking measurements

First of all, decide how wide you want the margins of the mount to be for the item being framed. Add an extra ½ in (12 mm) to the bottom margin for a better visual effect.

Tip

You can dramatise a tiny picture by giving it a wide mount.

1 *Measure the height and width of the picture, for example, 8 × 6 in (20 × 15 cm). Make the window slightly smaller than the picture, by subtracting ⅒ in (3 mm) per side from your measurements. The mount will cover these edges, and in this case the window will therefore measure 7⅘ × 5⅘ in (19.4 × 14.4 cm).*

2 To these measurements, add the dimensions of the mount margins, for example, 3 in (6 cm) on three sides and 3½ in (7 cm) for the margin beneath the window.

3 To obtain the measurements of the backing board, add the measurements of the window to the margins of the mount for the long and short sides:
7⅕ + 3 + 3 = 13⅖ in (19.4 + 6 + 6 = 31.4 cm);
5⅘ + 3 + 3½ = 12³⁄₁₀ in
(14.4 + 6 + 7 = 27.4 cm).

4 Cut the backing board to these dimensions.

Cutting the mount

1 Place the mountboard face down on the work surface. Place the backing board on it and draw round the perimeter with a pencil and ruler. Remove the backing board.

2 Cut the mountboard with the cutter against the heavy ruler. Check that it is exactly the same size as the backing board.

𝒯 𝒾 𝓅

For round, oval, octagonal or hexagonal windows, it's best to buy a mountboard ready cut with the desired window shape. To give a decorative finish to this type of mount, see page 119, 'Multiple photo mount with different-shaped windows'.

Cutting the window

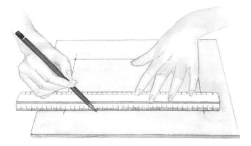

1 Mark the measurements of the mount margins on the back of the mountboard. Join the marks, overlapping the lines slightly at the corners.

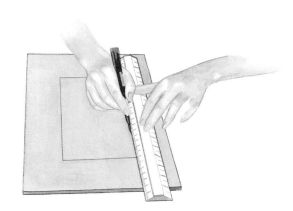

2 Lay the heavy ruler along the line and cut from one point to the next, making sure that the cutter doesn't go beyond the marks.

3 Remove the cut-out centre piece carefully, making sure you don't tear the card.

4 To ensure a neat cut, gently sand down the edges of the window with very fine glasspaper.

Positioning the mount

1 *Cut a piece of backing card the same size as the backing board.*

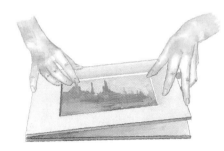

2 *Place the card, the picture and the mount on top of one other on the work surface.*

3 *Centre the picture within the window, holding it down with a weight. Gently remove the mount.*

4 *Cut a strip of brown gummed paper tape slightly shorter than the width of the picture. Use it to stick the picture to the card along one side, starting from the middle, overlapping the picture by 1/12 in (2 mm).*

5 *Place the mount over the subject and check that the tape does not show.*

Covering a mount

A mount may be covered in fabric or paper, and the method is the same whichever you use. Avoid using synthetic fabrics, or papers that are too thin. The instructions below are for covering a mount with paper.

MATERIALS

Mounting card	Heavy ruler
Bookbinding or other	Cutter
decorative paper	Fine pencil
PVA adhesive	Protective sheet of
Flat paintbrush	paper
Paper knife	Metal scale rule

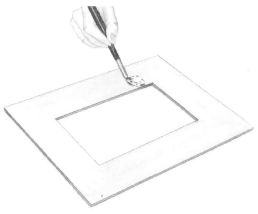

1 *Cut the mount to the dimensions of the backing board; refer to the previous instructions to cut the window.*

Tip

When cutting the window, take extra care with the corners to ensure that they are cleanly cut.

3 *Brush adhesive all over the surface of the mount, removing any excess from the corners of the window.*

2 *Cut a piece of decorative paper about 1 in (2.5 cm) larger all round than the mount.*

4 *Place the paper right side down on the work surface, and place the mount centrally on it, adhesive side down.*

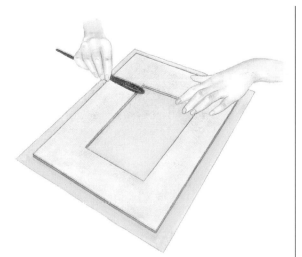

5 *Quickly smooth it down with the paper knife to remove any creases in the paper.*

Tip

It is important to stick the paper down
quickly, to avoid creasing it.
If creases appear, remove the paper
and moisten the right side of it evenly
with a damp sponge before reapplying.

6 *Turn the mount face up, cover with a protective sheet of paper and, with the paper knife held flat, smooth down the decorative paper firmly and evenly. Place it under a press for an hour.*

Tip

To form a press, place the decorated mount under
two pieces of backing board and place heavy
objects (such as books or flowerpots) on top. The
protective sheet of paper allows you to press the
mount without damaging the decorative paper.

7 *Take the mount from the press. Place it paper side down on the work surface. Using the cutter, cut a window in the paper, about 1 in (2.5 cm) in from the edges of the mount window. Remove the cut-away paper.*

8 *Using the cutter, make a 45° cut at each corner, starting from the mount window corners.*

9 *Brush adhesive on to one of these inner borders of the paper.*

10 *Working from the centre outwards, take this glued section of paper between thumb and index finger, and fold it over on to the back of the mount. Use the paper knife to smooth out any bumps.*

11 *Repeat steps 9 and 10 for the other three sides.*

12 *Place the heavy ruler on the outer edges of the mount and cut away the surplus paper.*

13 *Place the finished mount under the press overnight.*

Final assembly

The dimensions of the frame are always based on those of the backing board.

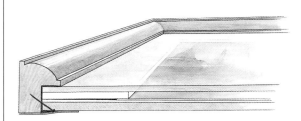

1 *Assemble the following elements: backing board, backing card with picture, mount and glass, spotlessly clean.*

2 *Refer to the section 'Simple picture framing: Final assembly' on pages 30–31, steps 2 to 14.*

FRAMING WITH SLIP MOUNTS

Slip mounts consist of two or three mounts one on top of the other, with each successive window wider than the one below it. As with bevelling, this technique enables you to give more depth to a subject, but it can also, with careful choice of colours and contrasts, help bring out a picture's colours.

MATERIALS

Backing board
Backing card
Decorative mounts in two different colours
Heavy ruler
Cutter
Fine pencil
Adhesive

Metal scale rule
Frame
1¾-in (4.5-cm) brown gummed paper tape
½-in (12-mm) pins
Damp sponge
Glass

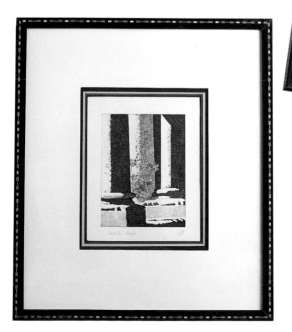

Taking measurements

The following method is for a slip made up of two mounts, but you can repeat the method for three mounts.
The first mount, or 'insert', is placed over the picture, and the second is put on top of it, and so on. To form the insert mount, refer to the section 'Framing with a mount' on page 32.

1 *The external measurements of the second mount, like the first, will be identical to those of the backing board. Cut it to size using the backing board as a pattern.*

2 *For this second mount, decide on the distance between the windows of the two mounts. For aesthetic reasons this should not be more than ¼ in (5 mm).*

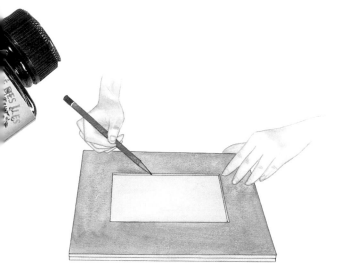

3 *For reference, and to help you visualise the difference between the two windows, place the first on the reverse side of the second and draw round the edge of the window, keeping the pencil perpendicular to the mountboard. Remove the first mount.*

4 *Using the pencil, measure and mark the corners of where you want the the second mount window to be.*

5 *Draw straight lines between the points, using the metal ruler.*

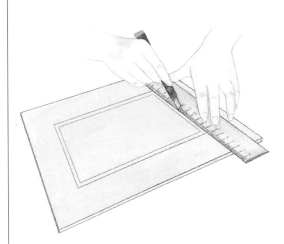

6 *Cut out the window of the second mount in the same way as the first.*

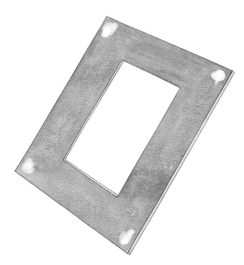

7 *Put the two mounts together, checking that their windows are straight and square. Apply a spot of adhesive to each outer corner of the upper surface of the insert mount. Position the second and smooth it down with the palm of your hand.*

8 *To position the picture behind the mounts, refer to the section 'Framing with a mount: Positioning the mount' on page 35, steps 1 to 5.*

THE GREAT INTERNATIONAL BOAT RACE, AUG. 27th, 1869

Tip

It's better to choose a darker shade for the first mount, to highlight the subject, and a lighter shade for the one above it, to add brightness. When choosing mount colours, pick a dominant colour in the picture itself, or one that harmonises with the decoration of your room (perhaps the main colour of the curtains or sofa, for example).

Final assembly

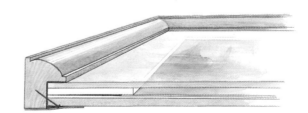

For the final assembly, refer to the section 'Framing with a mount: Final assembly' on page 38, steps 1 and 2.

Bevelling is the technique of making oblique cuts in the edges of a mount. It can be done using standard or extra thick mountboard (bevelling board), under or over a thin decorative mount, as in these examples. The resulting mount gives the picture surround a strongly defined finish. The bevelled edges themselves may be decorated with paper or fabric, or painted.

*B*EVELLING

MATERIALS

Backing board	Frame
Bevelling board	1¾-in (4.5-cm) brown
Heavy ruler	gummed paper tape
Scale rule	½-in (12-mm) pins
Paper knife	Damp sponge
45° set square	Glass
PVA adhesive	Mounting card
Fine glasspaper	Cutter
Bookbinding paper	Fine pencil
Pliers	

FRAMING WITH A BEVELLED WINDOW MOUNT

Cutting a bevelled edge with a ruler and cutter is a delicate operation. You should therefore practise with offcuts of board before making a final cut.
If picture framing becomes a favourite activity, it makes sense to invest in a mount cutter, which will enable you to cut perfect bevels easily.

Measuring and cutting

Before cutting bevelled edges, you need to make a decorative or coloured mount that will go over the top of the bevelled mount when you come to assemble your picture. Refer to the section 'Framing with a mount' on page 32 for calculating and cutting the decorative mount.

1 *When calculating the margins of this top mount, take account of the width of the bevels. Deduct ¼ in (5 mm) from the margin measurement for board ⅙ in (4 mm) thick, and ⅙ in (4 mm) for board ¹⁄₁₀ in (3 mm) thick.*

2 *Cut the window for the top mount using the measurements thus obtained. Cut the backing board to size.*

Tip

It is essential to practise cutting bevelled edges before making your first piece, using a new blade for each cut. To making bevelling simpler, use a mount cutter, a special cutter on a 45° angle with integral ruler.

3 *Transfer the dimensions of the backing board to the bevelling board. Cut this to size.*

4 Position the decorative mount on the bevelling board and use a pencil to mark the edges of the window.

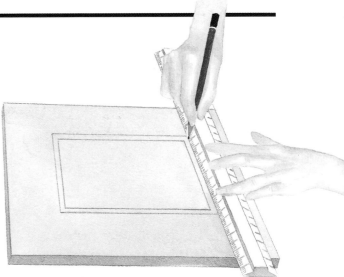

5 Remove the decorative mount and draw a second line ¹⁄₂₄ in (1 mm) outside the first one that marks the edge of the window.

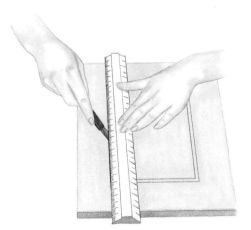

6 Place the heavy ruler to the left of the line on the right-hand side of the board, that is, just within the outer line. Hold the cutter at a 45° angle against the edge of the ruler. Cut from top to bottom, going slightly beyond the edge of the line at each end.

7 Repeat the cut several times, holding the cutter at exactly the same angle every time.

8 Repeat steps 6 and 7 for the three other sides.

Start the bevelled cuts with the shorter sides and finish with the longer ones.

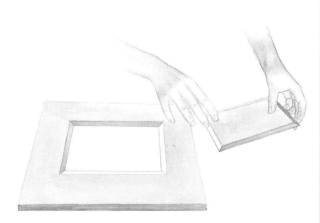

9 Carefully remove the central piece of board.

10 Lightly sand the bevels with fine glasspaper.

Covering the bevels

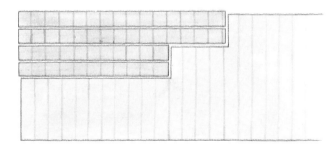

1 Cut four strips of bookbinding paper 1⅛ in (3 cm) wide and 1½ in (4 cm) longer than the relevant edges of the window. Ensure that the grain of the paper lies across the width of each strip rather than along it.

2 Fold each strip in half lengthways, pattern side inwards, and crease with the paper knife.

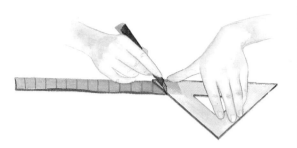

3 Place a strip on the work surface, position the 45° set square on the left-hand end of the strip and cut the left-hand end.

4 Place this strip on the back of the bevelled window, with the left-hand end of the paper extending ¹⁄₂₄ in (1 mm) beyond the corner. With a pencil, mark the other end of the strip ¹⁄₂₄ in (1 mm) beyond the other corner.

5 Cut this angle with the cutter, using the 45° set square.

6 Brush a 1-in (2.5-cm) wide strip of adhesive over the back edge of the mountboard, taking care not to put too much in the corners.

7 Stick the strip of bookbinding paper on to the adhesive along the edge of the window. Smooth down with the paper knife.

8 Turn the mountboard face up and apply adhesive to the bevel and to the first inch (2.5 cm) of the top surface of the mount.

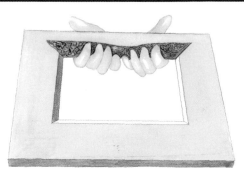

14 *Glue the strip in place, following the instructions in steps 6 to 10.*

15 *Repeat for the second short strip.*

Final assembly

1 *Cut a piece of backing card the same size as the backing board.*

2 *Place the card, the picture and the bevelled mount on the work surface.*

3 *Centre your picture within the window and weight it.*

4 *Remove the mount. Cut a small piece of brown gummed paper tape.*

5 *Use this tape to stick one edge of the picture to the card, overlapping the picture by no more than $1/12$ in (2 mm).*

6 *Carefully centre the bevelled mount under the decorative mount, making sure that the top mount does not cover the bevels.*

9 *Press the rest of the paper strip down over the bevel and the glued surface of the mount.*

10 *Smooth down the paper with the paper knife, taking particular care with the corners.*

11 *Apply the second long strip to the opposite edge, repeating these steps exactly.*

12 *Place the first short strip of bookbinding paper on the work surface, position the 45° set square at the left-hand end, and cut.*

13 *Place this strip on the back of the bevelled window, adjusting the left-hand angle to fit the corner of the window. Mark the other end of the strip with a pencil, lining it up precisely with the right-hand corner of the window. Cut this end with the set square.*

7 *Assemble the elements as follows: backing board, mounting card with picture, bevelled mount, decorative mount and finally the spotlessly clean glass.*

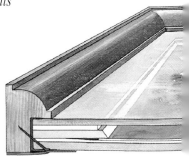

8 *Refer to the section 'Simple picture framing: Final assembly' on pages 30–31, steps 2 to 14. The size of the frame is always based on the dimensions of the backing board.*

FRAMING WITH REVERSE BEVELS

This technique will also give a picture more depth. Reverse bevels are cut from bevelling board, but in contrast to a classic bevelled window mount, the picture is mounted on top of the central portion. Its edges must be straight and the corners perfectly true. The bevels themselves may be finished with paper or fabric, or painted. In the example shown here, the backing card around the picture is covered with fabric and the bevelled edges are painted.

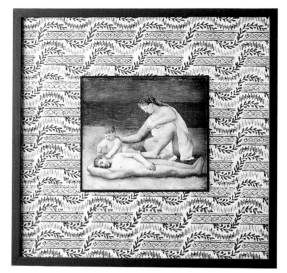

MATERIALS

Backing board	Fine glasspaper
Mounting card	2 flat paintbrushes
Bevelling board	Piece of fabric
Attachments	Paper knife
Strong brown adhesive tape	Clean cloth
Heavy ruler	Textured paint to
Cutter	match the fabric
Metal scale rule	4 weights
Fine pencil	

Measuring and cutting

First, determine the dimensions of the backing board.

1 Cut the backing board and mounting card to these dimensions.

2 To fix the hanging attachment to the backing board, refer to the section 'Simple picture framing: Fixing the hanging attachment' on page 26, steps 1 to 5.

3 Take a piece of bevelling board larger than your picture. Centre your picture on the board, and draw round it with a fine pencil held at 45°. Remove the picture.

4 Place a heavy ruler to the left of the board, just beyond the pencil line. Hold the cutter at a 45° angle against the edge of the ruler. Cut from top to bottom, extending the cut a little beyond each end of the line. Repeat several times to cut the full depth of the board.

5 Repeat step 4 for the other three sides.

6 Remove this central piece. Sand down the bevelled edges with glasspaper to make them smooth and clean.

Tip

Keep the cut-away surround to use later for a classic bevelled window mount.

Covering the mounting card and painting the bevels

1 Using the heavy ruler and cutter, cut a piece of fabric slightly larger than the mounting card.

2 Place the fabric face down on the work surface. Brush adhesive over the card, checking that there are no blobs, and place it carefully on the fabric without making creases.

3 Turn the covered card over and gently pull the edges of the fabric to stretch it. Smooth it out with the paper knife and a clean cloth, checking that there are no air bubbles. Leave to dry for an hour.

4 Place the card, fabric side down, on the work surface. Position the heavy ruler on the edges of the card, and trim away surplus fabric with the cutter.

Tip

Always use the cutter to trim fabric, as it will cut much more cleanly than scissors.

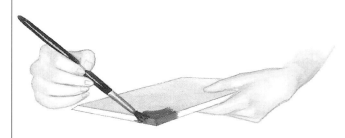

5 Paint all the bevels and the edge of the top surface of the board, which will be covered by your picture.

Final assembly

1 Brush adhesive over the backing board. Position the covered mounting card, plain side down, on the backing board, easing it carefully into place.

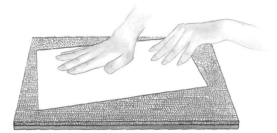

2 Cover with a protective sheet of paper and press down with your hand from top to bottom. Use the paper knife to remove surplus adhesive from the edges. Put it under a press.

5 Take the backing board from the press. Centre the bevelled mount on the backing board (fabric side up). Mark the position of the bevelled mount with weighted offcuts of board on the fabric-covered card.

6 Gently remove the bevelled mount, turn it over and apply adhesive to the back.

3 To stick the picture to the bevelled mount, cut four small pieces of brown gummed paper tape and fold them in half. Moisten half of each one and stick them to the back of the picture in each corner.

7 Replace the bevelled mount on the covered mounting card. Remove the weights and board offcuts, and reposition the weights on the bevelled mount. Leave to dry for an hour.

4 Moisten the other side of each piece of tape and position the picture on the mount, smoothing it out well.

8 For the final assembly, refer to the section 'Simple picture framing: Final assembly' on pages 30–31. Place the elements in the frame in the following order: glass, bevelled mount and backing board with hanging attachment.

RELIEF BEVELLED MOUNT

In relief bevelling, the picture is framed by a mount formed by a relief insert. Both the inner and outer edges of this mount are bevelled, and it is bordered by a low-level margin just inside the frame. It is essential to use thick bevelling board for the relief insert, which will be covered with a decorative finish.

Before undertaking this framing technique, carefully consider the subject to be framed and determine the appropriate widths of bevelled relief insert and the outer margin (between bevel and frame). To avoid mistakes, it's best to make a template from offcuts of thin card or paper. This will enable you to see the overall effect and, where necessary, alter the dimensions.

MATERIALS

Backing board	Fine glasspaper
Bevelling board	HB or H pencil
Mounting card with	Cutter
decorative finish	Hanging attachment
Heavy ruler	Brown gummed paper tape
Scale rule	Strong brown
Mount cutter	adhesive tape
Paper knife	Sponge
45° set square	Glass
PVA adhesive	½-inch (12-mm) pins

Preliminary measurements

For example, for a picture 7 × 10½ in (18 × 26 cm), deduct ½ in (2 mm) from each side – 6¹¹⁄₁₂ and 10⁵⁄₁₂ in (17.8 and 25.8 cm).

Relief margin, in bevelling board: 3½ in (7 cm) on all sides. Don't add ½ in (1 cm) for the bottom margin.

Bevelled edges: ¼ in (0.5 cm) for each bevel.

Outer margin between the bevelled edge of the relief margin and the frame: 2 in (5 cm) on each side.

The dimensions of the backing board are therefore:

Width: 6¹¹⁄₁₂ + ¼ in (4) + 3½ in (2) = 14¹¹⁄₁₂ in (17.8 + 0.5 cm (4) + 7 cm (2) + 5 cm (2) = 43.8 cm).

Height: 10⁵⁄₁₂ + ¼ in (4) + 3½ in (2) = 18⁵⁄₁₂ in (25.8 + 0.5 cm (4) + 7 cm (2) + 5 cm (2) = 51.8 cm).

Cut the backing board to these dimensions and fix the hanging attachment. Transfer the dimensions of the backing board to mounting card and cut this to size. This card will show as the margin between the reverse bevelled edge and the frame, and may be painted or covered.

4 Position the heavy ruler on the lines and cut between the points, ensuring that you do not go beyond the corners. Once the four sides have been cut, remove the central piece.

5 To ensure a neat cut, lightly sand the inner cut edges of the window with very fine glasspaper.

6 Place the backing board, mounting card and mount to one side to stop them getting damaged.

Measuring and cutting the bevelled mount

1 Take a piece of bevelling board the same size as the backing board and transfer to this the external dimensions of the decorative mount. Join these points. Position the mount cutter inside the lines and cut, going just beyond the ends of the lines. Cut this reverse bevel all round the board.

2 Place the decorative mount on the bevelling board and, using a pencil, trace the edges of the window opening. Remove the decorative mount and add ¹⁄₂₄ in (1 mm) all round to increase the size of the window.

3 To cut this bevelled window, place the mount cutter outside one of these lines. Cut along the line from top to bottom, going slightly beyond each end of the line. Repeat for the other three sides.

4 Remove the central piece of board and put it aside for another project.

Measuring and cutting the decorative mount

1 Take the dimensions of the picture – 6¹¹⁄₁₂ × 10⁵⁄₁₂ in (17.8 × 25.8 cm) – and add to these the width of the relief mount: 2 × 3½ in (7 cm).

2 Transfer these dimensions – 13¹¹⁄₁₂ × 17⁵⁄₁₂ in (31.8 × 39.8 cm) – to mounting card and cut out, using a heavy ruler and cutter.

3 Transfer the width of the margins of the relief mount (3½ in (7 cm)) to the back of the card. Join these points with a pencil line, overlapping slightly at the corners. Check that the widths of all the margins are equal.

5 *Position the decorative mount over the bevelled mount, making sure it fits exactly and does not cover the bevelled edges.*

6 *Lightly sand the bevels with fine glasspaper.*

Final assembly

1 *Position all the elements as follows: backing board, mounting card, picture, bevelled mount and decorative mount. Check that these are in the correct order.*

2 *Once everything is in place, assemble the frame as described in the section 'Simple picture framing: Final assembly' on pages 30–31.*

SUSPENDED MOUNT

With a suspended mount, the picture sits on a central raised mount with reverse bevels, surrounded by a wide sunken margin and an outer bevelled window mount. This gives the impression that the picture is floating within the frame.

It is important first to make a template from thin card or paper, to ensure that you have the correct dimensions for the margins and bevelled edges. For this, refer to the section 'Relief bevelled mount' on page 50.

MATERIALS

Backing board	Fine glasspaper
Bevelling board	HB or H pencil
Mounting card with	Cutter
decorative finish	Hanging attachment
Heavy ruler	Brown gummed
Scale rule	paper tape
Mount cutter	Strong brown adhesive tape
Paper knife	Sponge
45° set square	Glass
PVA adhesive	½-in (12-mm) pins

In this example the picture measures 9½ × 13 in (23 × 32 cm).
The sunken margin between the two bevelled edges is 3¼ in (8 cm). Don't make the bottom margin wider.
The decorative mount to cover the bevelled window mount is 2½ in (6 cm) wide on each side. Don't add any more for the bottom margin.
To calculate the dimensions of the backing board, add the dimensions of the picture, the margin

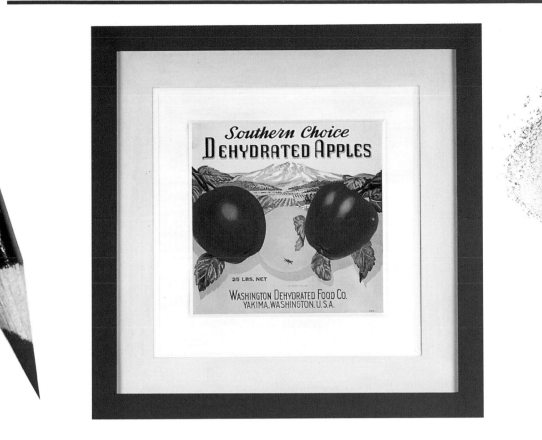

between the two bevelled edges and the margin of the window mount:
Width: 9½ + 3¼ in (2) + 2½ in (2) = 21 in
(23 + 8 cm (2) + 6 cm (2) = 51 cm.
Height: 13 + 3¼ in (2) + 2½ in (2) = 24½ in
(32 + 8 cm (2) + 6 cm (2) = 60 cm.
Cut the backing board to these dimensions and fix the hanging attachment. Transfer the same dimensions to mounting card and cut this to size. This will form the sunken margin between the two bevelled edges, and may be painted or covered in decorative paper.

Measuring and cutting the central bevelled mount

1 Take a piece of bevelling board bigger than the subject to be framed. Add ¹⁄₂₄ in (1 mm) to the dimensions of the picture, and transfer these

measurements to the board. Join the points with pencil lines.

2 Place a heavy ruler outside these lines and, holding the cutter at a 45° angle, cut each side from top to bottom, taking each cut just beyond each end of the lines. If you are using a mount cutter, place it inside the lines.

3 Remove the central piece. Sand the bevels with glasspaper, making sure that they are straight and true.

Measuring and cutting the decorative mount

1 Take a piece of mounting card and mark on it the dimensions of the backing board: 21 × 24½ in (51 × 60 cm). Join these points with a pencil line, and cut using the heavy ruler and the cutter.

2 Mark out the dimensions of the margin of the decorative mount (2½ in (6 cm)), starting from the exterior edge of the card, and cut out the window, taking care not to extend the cut beyond the corners.

Measuring and cutting the outer bevelled mount

1 Transfer the measurements of the backing board to a piece of bevelling board, and cut it to size.

2 Position the decorative mount over the board and mark in pencil the dimensions of the window.

3 Remove the decorative mount and add ½₄ in (1 mm) to widen the window.

4 Place the heavy ruler inside one of the lines drawn. Holding the cutter at a 45° angle against the ruler, cut from top to bottom, taking the cut just beyond the lines. If using a mount cutter, place this outside the lines.

5 Repeat this cut on the other three sides of the board.

Final assembly

1 Position all the elements as follows: backing board, mounting card, the subject mounted on the central bevelled mount and the bevelled window mount covered with the decorative mount. Check that these are all correct.

2 Once you have checked that everything is in place, assemble the frame as described in the section 'Simple picture framing: Final assembly' on pages 30–31.

The bevelled edges and the mount, if made from mounting card, may be covered with paper or fabric, or painted.

FRAMING WITH AN OCTAGONAL BEVELLED MOUNT

An octagonal window mount inside a rectangular frame can give a lovely original effect, although it is quite a difficult technique to master. Specialist picture-framing suppliers may have mounts ready cut with octagonal windows, but these will obviously be of certain specific sizes, so make sure you take the subject you wish to frame with you.

MATERIALS

Backing board	Fine pencil
Bevelling board	Cutter
Mounting card with	Fine glasspaper
decorative finish	Paper knife
Bookbinding paper	45° set square
Heavy ruler	PVA adhesive
Scale rule	Cloth

Measuring and cutting the decorative mount

1 *Measure the height and width of the subject to be framed, for example: 8 × 12 in (20 × 28 cm). Deduct ¹⁄₁₀ in (3 mm) to give the size of the window: 7⅘ × 11⅘ in (19.4 × 27.4 cm).*

2 *Add to this the width of the margins of the mount: for example 3 in (7 cm) on all sides of the subject. When calculating the margins of the mount covering,, make sure you take into account the width of the bevelled edges. Deduct ¼ in (5 mm) from the dimensions of the margins for board ⅙ in (4 mm) thick and ⅙ in S(4 mm) for board ¹⁄₁₀ in (3 mm) thick.*
7⅘ + 6 = 13⅘ in (19.4 + 14 = 33.4 cm);
11⅘ + 6 = 17⅘ in (27.4 + 14 = 41.4 cm).
These measurements are for the backing board and the outer edges of the mount.

3 *Transfer the dimensions of the margins to the back of the mount and draw a line between the points, overlapping slightly at the corners.*

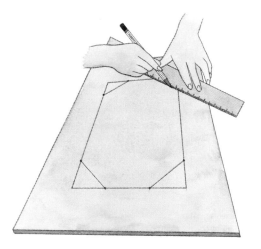

4 *Having drawn a rectangle in this way, position your scale rule along one of the short sides and mark the starting point of an oblique line which will cross each corner of the rectangle to give the octagonal shape.*

5 *Mark this measurement – say 2 in (5 cm) – in pencil eight times, in each direction from each of the corners of the window. Join these points, marking an oblique line across each corner to create an octagon.*

6 *Position the heavy ruler against one of these diagonal lines. Cut with the cutter, taking care not to go beyond the ends of the line. Repeat for each of the eight sides.*

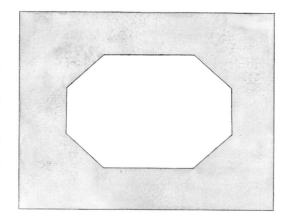

7 *Remove the central piece and lightly sand the cut edges of the window smooth with fine glasspaper.*

8 *Cut the rectangular backing board to the dimensions obtained previously: 13⅘ × 17⅘ in (33.4 cm × 41.4 cm).*

Tip

You can of course make an octagonal window mount without bevelled edges.

Tip

It's best to use a mount cutter to bevel an octagonal window, since the angles of all eight bevels must be identical; if they differ slightly it will be immediately obvious. Cutting with a mount cutter is also quicker.

Measuring and cutting the octagonal bevelled window

1 *Transfer the measurements of the backing board to the bevelling board and cut to size.*

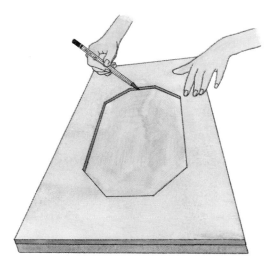

2 *Place the decorative mount on the bevelling board and trace the shape of the octagon with a pencil.*

3 *Remove the decorative mount and increase the window size by 1/24 in (1 mm).*

4 *Bevel the edges as described in the section 'Bevelling: Measuring and cutting' on pages 42–4.*

Covering the decorative mount and the bevelled edges

For the decorative mount, refer to the section 'Multiple picture mounts with different shaped windows' on page 119, and follow the step-by-step instructions.

For the bevelled edges, refer to the section 'Bevelling: Measuring and cutting' on pages 42–4, and follow the step-by-step instructions.

Most frames are rectangular, square or round, but you need not be limited to these traditional shapes. In the Victorian era the fashion was for octagonal frames, particularly for mirrors. This type of frame works well with a mount with a rectangular, oval or round window.

ORNAMENTAL FRAMES

MATERIALS

Frame moulding	Mounting card or
Emery board	mountboard
Clamp	1¾-in (4.5-cm) brown
Paintbrush	gummed paper tape
Wood glue	Paper knife
Cloth	Sponge
Backing board	Glass
Heavy ruler	½-in (12-mm) pins
Scale rule	Mitre saw
Fine pencil	(recommended)
Cutter	

POLYGONAL FRAMES

For polygonal frames it's best to use a proper mitre saw, which will ensure precise cutting of the angles. This example shows you how to make an octagonal frame. To determine the angle of each corner, simply divide 180° by eight, which makes each angle 22.5°. This formula can be adapted for any polygonal frame style. You will need to use separate clamps to assemble this type of frame.

Cutting and assembly

1 Work out where you will make your cuts for each section of the frame, using the formula explained in the introduction above. Position the blade of the mitre saw at the chosen angle and cut the required number of moulding pieces.

2 Once the cuts have been made, gently sand each angle with an emery board.

3 Fix the clamp to the work table. Open it sufficiently to allow two cut pieces to be inserted.

4 Take two pieces of moulding, and brush wood glue on to the angles of the ends to be joined.

5 Place the sections in the clamp, glued ends pressed together, and tighten the clamp. Remove excess glue with a damp cloth. Allow to set for about an hour.

Tip
When assembling the frame, using several individual clamps will speed up the process.

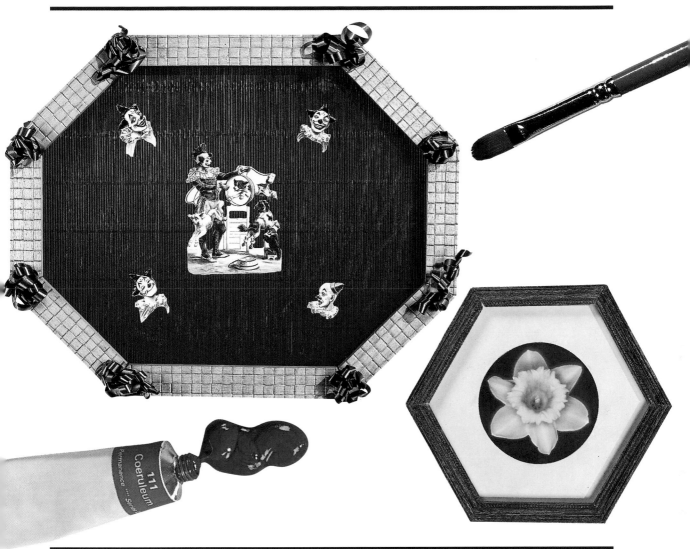

6 Take the two joined pieces from the clamp. Take a third piece of moulding, apply glue to the angle to be joined and to the other end of one of the pieces already joined. Clamp as before.

7 Repeat for all the moulding pieces until the frame is complete.

8 Put the frame to one side and leave to set for two to three hours.

Tip
Placing the frame face down on the work surface will enable you to measure its interior dimensions for cutting out the backing board.

Cutting the backing board and mount

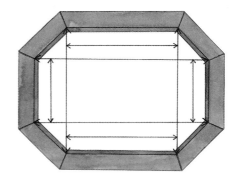

1 Use the scale rule to measure the interior dimensions of the frame.

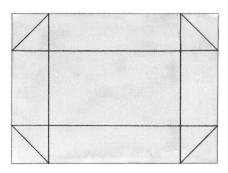

2 *Transfer these dimensions to the backing board using the ruler and a pencil.*

3 *Cut the backing board to size, using the cutter and heavy ruler.*

Tip

If using ready-finished mountboard, draw the pencil lines on the wrong side.

4 *To make the mount, place the cut-out backing board over the mounting card or mountboard on the work surface. Draw round the backing board with the pencil.*

5 *Remove the backing board and, using the cutter and heavy ruler, cut the card or mountboard to size. Check that the two octagons are identical.*

6 *Cut out your chosen window as explained in the section 'Framing with a mount: Cutting the Window' on page 34.*

Final assembly

The final assembly of a polygonal frame is identical to that of a classic frame. Refer to the section 'Simple picture framing: Final Assembly' on pages 30–31.

ANTIQUE-STYLE PICTURE FRAMING

This framing technique is used for paintings on canvas stretched over a wooden frame. The canvas is surrounded by a 'slip', an extra frame of wood between the canvas and the outer frame. You can make a slip frame wide or narrow, using flat or sloping pieces of wood, but the base of the timber must be flat to allow the outer frame to butt up against it. Slip frames may be finished with fabric (generally linen, thick cotton or velvet) or painted. The following instructions are for a painted slip with a decorative frame moulding.

MATERIALS

Slip frame	Outer frame
Mitre box	Moulding
Saw	Wood glue
Moulding	Mountboard or hardboard
Emery board	offcut
Wood glue	PVA adhesive
Cord clamp	½-in (12-mm) pins
Metal scale rule	1½-in and 2¾-in (4-cm and
Pencil	7-cm) nails
Fine glasspaper	Hammer
Flat paintbrushes	Bradawl
Clean cloth	2 screw eyes
Damp sponge	Cord
Textured paint, in a colour	Pliers
complementary to the	1¾-in (4.5-cm) brown
painting	gummed paper tape

Measuring, cutting and assembling the slip frame

1 *Place the canvas on its stretcher on the work surface. Measure the length and width of the canvas in several places. Note the longest of these dimensions, but don't add the usual ½ in (2 mm) play to the dimensions obtained.*

2 *Cut the slip frame according to the instructions in 'Simple picture framing: Measuring, cutting and assembling the moulding' on pages 27–8, steps 2 to 7.*

3 *Sand each cut angle with the emery board.*

4 *Assemble the cut ends using the cord clamp, following the instructions on page 29, steps 9 to 12. Leave to set for three hours.*

5 *Once it has set, remove the cord clamp and wipe any excess glue from the corners with a damp sponge and cloth.*

6 *Sand down the top, back and corners of the slip frame with glasspaper until the wood is quite smooth.*

T i p

Check that there are no imperfections on the slip frame. Fill any small gaps at the corners with wood filler and sand down again. Use a damp sponge to remove all splinters and sawdust caused by the sanding. If you are covering the slip frame with fabric, lightly sand the moulding.

7 Place the slip frame on the work surface, so that one side hangs over the edge slightly.

8 Paint this side of the slip frame, starting with the lip, then the top, then the back. Turn it round and repeat for the other three sides. Apply two or three coats of paint. Allow to dry for three hours.

T i p

When painting the slip, apply the paint smoothly and evenly. Start from one corner and proceed towards the next, without going back over your work and building up too thick a layer of paint.

Measuring, cutting and assembling the outer frame

1 Measure the outside edges of the slip frame. Add ¹⁄₁₂ in (2 mm) play to these dimensions.

2 Refer to the instructions for measuring, cutting and assembling the frame on pages 27–9, steps 2 to 14.

Final assembly

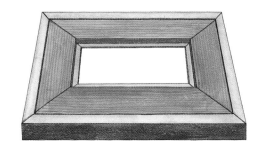

1 Place the outer frame face down on the work surface and insert the slip frame into it.

2 From mountboard or hardboard offcuts, cut out four triangular pieces large enough to hold the slip in place in the outer frame.

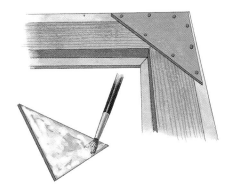

3 Apply glue to the back of each of these four triangles, and stick one on each corner of the outer frame. Tack them in place with pins.

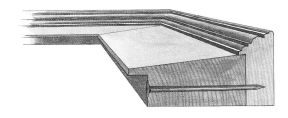

4 Nail the slip frame to the outer frame with 1½-in (4-cm) nails, through the vertical face of the rebate on all four sides.

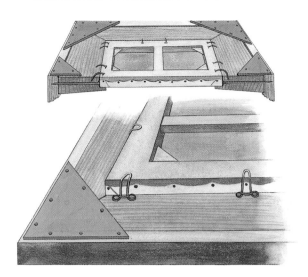

5 *Position the canvas within the slip frame. Nail 2¾-in (7-cm) nails halfway into the base of the slip frame at 4-in (10-cm) intervals. Fold them down at right angles with a pair of pliers, so that they rest against the back of the stretcher.*

6 *Make a mark with a bradawl three-quarters of the way up each side of the back of the moulding. Enlarge the holes with the bradawl. Screw an eye into each hole until tight. String a cord or picture wire between the two eyes, and hang on the wall.*

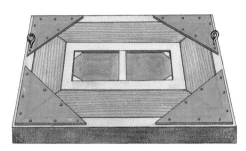

Tip

When using a bradawl to make the hole, take care not to split the wood of the moulding.

Tip

If the back of the stretcher is not at the same level as that of the slip frame, use four clip fasteners instead of long nails. Screw these into the back of the slip frame, in the centre of all four sides, and bend the top of each clip over the back of the stretcher. The tension of the clips holds the canvas in place in the slip frame.

FRAMING A CANVAS WITH A VALLEY SURROUND

This type of framing involves placing a flat wooden backing – which forms a trough, or valley – between the canvas and the frame, giving an impression of space and setting off the painting. Timber battens or small planks are used, depending on the width of the required valley. The valley may be painted or covered with mounting card, which may in turn be decorated with fabric or paper. This is cut to fit the valley and glued in place. The outer frame surrounding the valley is at the same level as the stretcher, or slightly higher. Use a plain moulding for the frame, which you can paint the same colour as the valley. The example described in this section is made using a painted valley 3 in (7.5 cm) wide and a plain moulding.

MATERIALS

Valley	Outer frame
Mitre box	Plain moulding in natural
Saw	wood
4-in (10-cm) wide battens	Protective fabric
Emery board	½-in (12-mm) nails
Wood glue	Bradawl
Cord clamp	2 screw eyes
Metal scale rule	Cord
Pencil	
Fine glasspaper	
2 flat paintbrushes	
Clean cloth	
Damp sponge	
Textured paint that goes with the painting	
¾-in and 1-in (18-mm and 25-mm) nails	

Measuring the valley

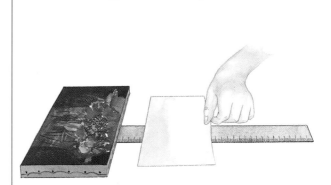

1 *Place the canvas face up on the work surface. Position the ruler against the side of the stretcher. Take a piece of paper to represent the frame and move it along the ruler until you have decided on the width of your valley.*

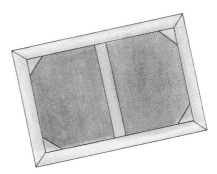

2 *Measure the width of the stretcher and add it to the measurements chosen for the valley (for example, 3 in + 1 in (7.5 cm + 2.5 cm)). Add a further inch (2.5 cm) to obtain the final width of the batten; this will be covered by the base of the outer frame moulding when the picture is assembled.*

3 *Measure the interior height and width of the stretcher (for example, 8 × 12 in (20 × 30 cm)). Add these two numbers and multiply by two: 40 in (100 cm). To this measurement add the width of the batten × 8 (here, 8 × 5 in = 40 in (8 × 12.5 cm = 100 cm)), giving a total of 80 in (200 cm). Allow 4 in (10 cm) spare; this means buying a total batten length of 84 in (210 cm).*

In the trade, battens are sold in 6-ft (2-m) lengths. For this type of frame buy the batten in standard lengths; you will always find a use for the offcuts.

3 Remove the cord clamp, and wipe any excess glue from the corners with a damp sponge and cloth. Nail each corner.

Cutting and assembling the valley

1 Cut the battens using the mitre box and saw. Do the long sides first, and then the shorter sides, following the instructions on page 28, steps 3 to 8. Position the battening in the mitre box with marked sides up.

2 Assemble the cut pieces in the cord clamp, following the instructions on page 29, steps 9 to 12. Leave to set for three hours.

Measuring, cutting and assembling the outer frame

1 The measurements used to determine the size of the outer frame in this example are 11 × 15 in (26 × 36 cm). Do not include the inch (2.5 cm) of the stretcher or the inch (2.5 cm) to be covered by the base of the frame during final assembly. Add ¹/₁₂ in (2 mm) play to these measurements, to give 11¹/₁₂ × 15¹/₁₂ in (26.2 × 36.2 cm).

2 Cut and assemble the outer frame, following the instructions on pages 27–9, steps 2 to 13.

Attaching the valley to the frame

1 *Place the outer frame face down on the work surface. Position the inner frame on the base of the outer frame. Before nailing together, check that the battening is properly centred in the outer frame.*

2 *Nail together with 1-in (25-mm) nails every 2 in (5 cm).*

3 *Turn the assembled frame over. Paint the valley and inside of the frame in your chosen colour. Leave to dry for three hours.*

Final assembly – attaching the canvas

1 *Cover the work surface with a protective cloth and place the canvas face down on it.*

2 *Position the assembled frame face down over the stretcher of the canvas, and nail together with ¾-in (18-mm) nails about every 1 ½ in (4 cm).*

3 *Fix screw eyes to the outer frame according to the instructions on page 63, step 6.*

FRAMING WITH TWO MOULDINGS

An original way of framing is to use two different mouldings, forming a kind of slip frame. It can be fun to mix styles of moulding in a project. For example, you might choose a cane moulding to go with a textured one, or one plain and one sloping, two or even three plain mouldings with one of them inverted, or a fancy gold leaf one with a plainer one. Natural wood mouldings may be used, and painted in different colours. Any kind of style is possible. You can add an extra touch of originality with a decorative or bevelled mount.

Materials

2 kinds of moulding	Metal hanging ring
Pins	Heavy ruler
Brown gummed paper tape	Cutter
Backing board	Wood glue
Scale rule	Glass

Method

Each frame is made separately.

1 *First, put together the elements which will form the package – picture, backing board, glass and so on – following the instructions in the relevant sections.*

2 *Using the measurements of the package, start by making up the first, or slip, frame, following the instructions on pages 28–9, steps 3 to 14.*

3 *For the second frame, take the outer dimensions of the first. Don't add any extra amount for play, since the slip frame must lie tight against the outer frame. Cut and assemble the mouldings, again following the instructions on pages 28–9.*

4 *Place the outer frame face down on the work surface. Position the slip frame inside it. Turn the whole frame over and check that the two elements fit snugly together.*

5 *Nail the frames together, inserting pins at regular intervals along the vertical faces of the rebate of the slip frame.*

Tip

Before nailing the frames together, check that you are using the correct length of pin. Use fine, headless pins. Where necessary use a nail punch.

6 *Place the package within the double frame, and carry out the final assembly.*

Framing a picture between two pieces of glass is an aesthetically pleasing technique that gives a light, airy impression and suits all kinds of subject. If the item is valuable it's better to mount it on backing card or bevelling board first. Many variations are possible on the double-glazing theme.

DOUBLE-GLAZED FRAMING

MATERIALS

Frame
Two identical pieces of glass, ½ in (2 mm) thick
Balsa mouldings
Neoprene glue
1 screw eye

Metal scale rule
Cutter
Double-sided adhesive tape
Bradawl
Spotlessly clean cloth

A SIMPLE DOUBLE-GLAZED FRAME

Use fairly plain frame mouldings that are not too wide, to keep the whole effect light. The rebate should be at least ½ in (12 mm) deep, to accommodate two layers of glass and the lengths of balsa wood used to fix the glass to the frame. The balsa is cut to length with the cutter and positioned against the rebate. The picture is hung with a screw eye attachment.

Method

1 *Place the item for framing on the work surface. Place the ruler against its edge and decide on the width of the margins. Don't forget to add an extra ½ in (12 mm) for the bottom margin. For example, given a subject of 6 × 8 in (15 × 20 cm), add 1½ in (4 cm) for the side and top margins and 2 in (5 cm) for the bottom margin. Cut the glass to the following dimensions: 6 + 1½ + 1½ in = 9 in (15 + 4 + 4 cm = 23 cm), and 8 + 1½ + 2 in = 11½ in (20 + 4 + 5 = 29 cm).*

Tip

If the item to be framed is very fragile, cut a piece of plain card very slightly smaller than the subject. Apply dots of glue to the corners of the card and fix the item to it. Alternatively, make up a reverse bevelled mount (see pages 47–9), remembering to smooth off the bevelled edges before attaching the item.

2 *Cut the frame mouldings to the exact measurements of the glass, to ensure that the glass will fit snugly in the frame. This example measures 9 × 11½ in (23 cm × 29 cm). Make the frame as described in 'Simple picture framing: Measuring, cutting and assembling the moulding', on pages 27–9, steps 1 to 14.*

*3 Place the frame face down on the work
surface. Using the cutter, cut the balsa
moulding to the length of the two longer sides,
then the other two sides.*

*4 Stain or paint the balsa moulding to match the
frame.*

*5 Take one of the pieces of glass, spotlessly clean.
Place it in the frame, and set it to one side.*

*6 Place your picture face down on the work
surface. Cut two small pieces of double-sided
adhesive tape. Remove the backing tape from one
of the sides and stick the pieces to the top and
bottom of the picture.*

*7 Clean the second piece of glass and place it
on a piece of non-felt cloth.*

8 Centre the subject, face up, on the second piece of glass and place a weight on it to hold it in place. Check the width of the margins. Do not remove the weight.

9 When the picture is centred, gently lift its top edge and remove the second backing strip from the adhesive tape. Gently press down with your hand. Repeat for the bottom edge.

10 Check that the glass in the frame is clean. Take the glass to which the picture is fixed by the edges and very gently place it in the frame, with the picture side against the first piece of glass.

Tip

When sticking the cut pieces of balsa moulding to the frame, it is best to start with the longer sides.

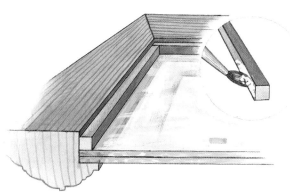

11 Apply neoprene glue to two sides of one of the pieces of balsa moulding. Position it against the rebate of the frame and the glass. Gently press along its length, ensuring that the balsa is in contact with both glass and rebate.

Tip

Remove all traces of excess glue with a cloth immediately, as it dries very quickly.

12 Repeat with the three other balsa mouldings. Allow to dry for an hour before moving.

13 Fix the screw eye to the back of the frame at the top. Make a central hole with the bradawl and screw in the eye. If the frame is too heavy for this, fix a screw eye to each vertical side.

Tip

Don't use cord to hang the frame, as this will be seen, but hang each eye from a nail.

DOUBLE GLAZING WITH A PAPER FRAME

A double-glazed picture with a decorative paper frame is a very simple, inexpensive way of framing a subject. The paper used is gummed, and many kinds are available from artists' suppliers, including marbled and geometric designs, gold and silver, plain colours and fabric effects.

MATERIALS

Subject	Hanging system
2 identical pieces of glass,	Backing board
½ in (2 mm thick)	Felt-tip pen
Metal scale rule	1¾-in (4.5-cm) brown
Cutter	gummed paper tape
Double-sided adhesive tape	White glue
Paper knife	Metal hanging ring
Very clean cloth	
½-in (12 mm) wide strips of	
gummed decorative paper	
Sponge	

Method

1 *Place the item to be framed on the work surface. Using the ruler, calculate the width of the margins you want (see page 68, step 1).*

2 *To fix your picture in place on the glass, cut two small pieces of double-sided adhesive tape and remove the backing tape from one side of each one. Stick these pieces to the back of the picture at top and bottom.*

3 *Place a piece of glass, carefully cleaned, on the work surface. Position your picture, face up, on the glass, and put a weight on it to hold it in place. Check with the ruler that the picture is central, and adjust its position if necessary.*

4 *When the subject is centred, gently lift its top edge and remove the second backing strip from the adhesive tape. Gently press down with your hand. Repeat for the bottom edge.*

5 *Thoroughly clean the second piece of glass, and check that both pieces are spotlessly clean. If necessary rub over again with a soft cloth, before placing the second piece on the first.*

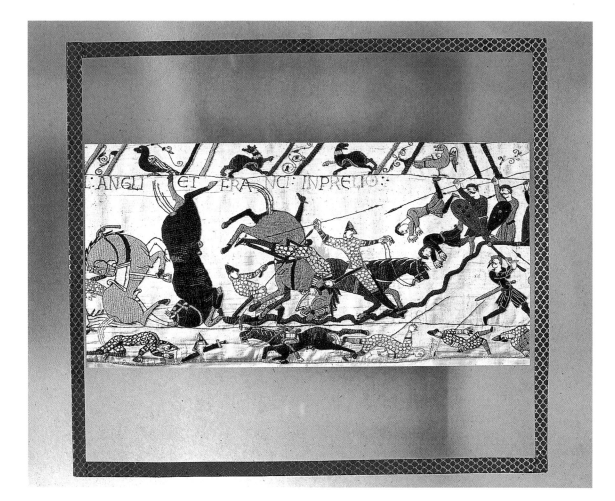

6 Place a cloth on the glass, and then a weight. Move the whole thing to the edge of the table until one side hangs over it. This makes it easier to apply the decorative paper.

7 Cut a piece of paper the length of the side overhanging the edge of the table.

8 To help with positioning, draw a dotted line along the paper ⅒ in (3 mm) from one edge. Place the ruler over the dots, and use the paper knife to fold up this narrow strip. Crease the fold.

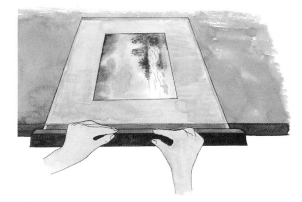

9 Moisten the back of the paper with a damp sponge. Stick the narrow edge to the top of the glass, gently pressing down with the thumbs from the centre towards the edges.

10 Without moving the glass, smooth the paper over the edge of it, and round to the back.

11 *Turn the picture round so that the opposite side to the side just finished hangs over the edge of the table. Repeat steps 7 to 10. Then finish the two other sides in the same way.*

The hanging system

If you want to hang this type of frame on a wall, you have to make a support for the hanging attachment that will be hidden behind the picture.

1 *Measure the picture inside the glass, and subtract ¾ to 1 in (18 to 25 mm) from these measurements for the backing board. This will ensure that the backing board to which the attachment will be fixed will not be visible.*

2 *Cut a piece of backing board to these dimensions and affix a piece of cord using two pieces of brown gummed paper tape, as shown in the last illustration.*

3 *Place the picture face down on the work surface. Centre the backing board on the glass and draw round the edge with a felt-tip pen. Remove the board.*

4 *Fill the area outlined with strips of brown gummed paper tape, stuck down side by side in one direction and then the other, forming a grid pattern. Remove any air bubbles with the paper knife after applying each strip. Leave to dry.*

5 *Apply white glue to the underside of the backing board, and stick it to the area of paper tape. Weight the corners and the centre, and leave to dry for about an hour.*

SUSPENDED DOUBLE-GLAZED FRAME

This type of double-glazed frame will make a picture seem to hang in thin air, giving a quite spectacular effect. It's quick and easy to make, although it's important to note that if you use superglue to fix together the two pieces of glass, you won't be able to change the picture once it is framed.

MATERIALS

Two pieces of glass of the same size, ½ in (2 mm) thick
Two corks
White paint

Superglue or strips of brown gummed paper tape
Cutter
Metal-scale rule
Cloth

Method

1 *Place your picture on the work surface. Using the ruler, calculate the width of the margins you want. Add these to the measurements of the picture. The example here is 8 × 5½ in (20 × 14 cm):*
8 + 3¼ + 3¼ = 14½ in (20 + 8 + 8 = 36 cm);
5½ + 3¼ + 3¾ = 12½ in (14 + 8 + 9 = 31 cm).

2 *Cut the two pieces of glass to these dimensions and clean them thoroughly.*

Tip

To make sure that the glass is spotless, hold it by the edges up to the light. Clean with a non-felt cloth.

3 *Place one piece of glass on the work surface. Place the picture face down on it and centre it. Hold it in place with a weight and check the width of the margins with the ruler.*

4 *Once the picture is centred, place a tiny dot of superglue on the four corners of the glass. Alternatively, apply a band of moistened gummed brown paper tape all the way round the edges of the two pieces of glass. Cut away the edges of the tape so that it only sticks to the cut edges of the glass.*

Tip

Take great care when applying super glue, as it sticks to the skin in seconds. Follow the instructions on the tube exactly.

5 *Take the second clean piece of glass and gently place it on top of the first. Don't slide the glass into place as the glue sets very quickly. Press on the corners over the dots of glue. Wait a few seconds for the glue to set.*

6 *Using the cutter, cut the corks into four ¾-in (18 mm) discs. Paint them with two coats of white paint.*

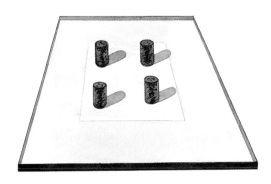

7 *Take one of the cork discs and apply a drop of superglue to the centre. Stick it behind one of the corners of the subject where it will not be seen. Press down for several seconds. Repeat with the other three corks.*

8 *The picture is hung on the wall using superglue. Apply glue to the centre of each cork disc and press the picture on to the wall. Maintain the pressure for about a minute.*

DOUBLE-GLAZED FRAME ON A BASE

This type of frame enables you to frame two pictures of the same size back to back. A wide range of bases, into which the glass is set, is possible, from a beautiful piece of wood such as chestnut or walnut, to stone or Perspex. Let your imagination run free!

You can place the frame on a table where the first picture can be seen from one side and the second from the other. The two pieces of glass are held together at the top by a plastic or metal clip. This design gives maximum effect for minimum time and outlay. In this example the base is of wood, which gives a natural effect.

MATERIALS

2 pieces of glass of the same size, ½ in (2 mm) thick
Metal or plastic clip

Base of wood or other material
Metal scale rule

Method

1 *Measure the items to be framed. In this example they are 6½ × 5 in (16 × 12.5 cm). Place the ruler against the edge of one of the pictures and decide on the width of the margins, in this case 2 in (5 cm). Add ½ in (12 mm) to the bottom margin as this will be set into the base.*

2 *Cut the glass, or have it cut, to the required dimensions, 9 × 7 in (22.2 × 17.5 cm).*

3 *Have a base cut from wood, 2 in (5 cm) thick, 7 in (17.5 cm) long and 3 in (7.5 cm) wide. Have a groove cut down the centre of the base, ⅛ in (4 mm) wide and ½ in (12 mm) deep.*

Tip

If the base is of wood, the groove is cut with a jigsaw. But whatever the chosen material, it is better to obtain the services of a specialist. You can paint the base in a colour of your choice or leave it natural.

4 *Carefully clean the two pieces of glass. Place the first on a clean cloth. Place the pictures back to back and centre them on the glass. Place the second piece of glass over the top.*

5 *Fasten the top of the frame with the clip and slide it into the base.*

Tip

Once everything is in place, keep the two pieces of glass firmly pressed together to ensure that the pictures don't slide out of position when you insert the glass into the base.

Pastels are a very delicate, fragile medium, so they should never touch the glass of a frame. There are several methods of framing pastels. The first is to use a window mount with or without a bevelled edge. The second consists of using a balsa moulding glued in place behind the frame moulding, against the rebate and the glass.

FRAMING PASTELS

FRAMING WITH A BACKING BOARD

Tip

Balsa mouldings come in various thicknesses, so measure the width and depth of the moulding rebate before buying. Make sure that the balsa will not be too deep for the rebate, taking account of the thickness of the backing board, usually $\frac{1}{10}$ or $\frac{1}{8}$ in (3 or 4 mm). For big pictures, choose a frame moulding with a large rebate. In addition, when buying mouldings and glass, have them cut and assembled by your supplier. Use $\frac{1}{10}$-in (3-mm) thick glass for pictures bigger than 48 × 32 in (120 cm × 80 cm)

MATERIALS

Backing board   Cutter
Frame moulding   PVA adhesive
Balsa moulding   Paint for the moulding
Glass   (optional)
Stapler   Paper knife
1¾-in (4.5-cm) brown   2 screw eyes
gummed paper tape   Cord
Clean cloth   Bradawl

Method

1 *Measure the pastel to be framed, in this example 48 × 32 in (120 × 80 cm). Cut a piece of backing board to these same measurements. Cut and assemble the mouldings and glass.*

Tip

Balsa mouldings are generally sold in 5-ft (1.50-m) lengths. Choose a colour to harmonise with the picture. If the right colour is not available, choose a natural wood moulding and paint in your chosen colour.

2 *Very gently place the pastel face down on a work surface, and place the backing board over it. Staple the top edge of the backing board to the pastel with three staples, to stop it slipping.*

3 *Put a clean cloth over the work surface and place the glass on it. Make sure that the glass is spotlessly clean.*

Tip

When cleaning a large piece of glass,
place it on the work surface with one
side hanging over the edge. This will
enable you to turn it more easily,
by holding each side and rocking it over
the edge of the table. To check that it is
completely clean, bend down so your eyes
are level with the work surface.

4 *On your spotlessly clean work surface, place
the frame face down and very carefully insert
the glass.*

Tip

With large pictures and frames,
get someone to help you install
the glass in the frame.

5 *Lay the length of balsa moulding on the glass
against the rebate of one of the long sides.
Using the cutter, mark where to cut it. It should
be exactly the same length as the side of the
frame. Cut the surplus with the cutter. Repeat for
the other three sides.*

Tip

Cut the balsa moulding for the longer
sides first, then the shorter ones.
If necessary, paint it the same colour
as the frame so that it doesn't show
in the finished frame.

6 *Apply glue to the wider face of the moulding,
which will be placed against the glass, then
the narrower side, which will lie against the
rebate.*

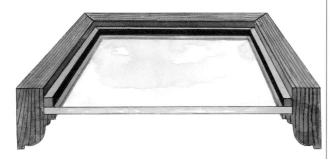

7 *Place the balsa moulding in the frame, glued
sides against the glass and the rebate. Press
into place with your index fingers along the
rebate and glass, your thumbs on the back of the
frame. Maintain pressure for several minutes.*

8 *Proceed in the same way for the other long
side, then for the two shorter sides. Remove
surplus glue with the tip of the paper knife and a
cloth.*

Tip

If the moulding is not firmly glued
to the rebate and the glass,
simply repeat the operation. If the
surplus glue does not come off easily,
gently scratch it off with the cutter.

9 *Position the pastel and the backing board in
the frame, and assemble the picture as
described in the section 'Simple picture
framing: Final assembly' on page 31,
steps 10–14.*

10 *On the back of one side of the frame,
make a mark with the bradawl about
8 in (20 cm) from the top and in the centre of
the moulding. Make a shallow pilot hole, then
screw an eye into the hole until firmly in
place. Repeat on the opposite side. Tie a cord
between the two eyes and hang the picture
on the wall.*

*To frame a pastel with a mount, refer to the
step-by-step instructions in the sections
'Framing with a mount' on page 32 or 'Framing
with a bevelled window mount' on page 42.*

FRAMING WITH A PLYWOOD BACKING

If your picture is bigger than the size of the largest backing board available, you will need to use plywood backing. In this example the plywood overlaps the back of the frame by ¾ in (18 mm). The frame's hanging system should be augmented by small metal angle brackets fixed to the wall to support the base of the frame.

MATERIALS

Plywood	Hammer
Glass	Nails
Frame moulding	Wood glue
Balsa mouldings	Mountboard offcuts
Bradawl	2 screw eyes
Screws	Cord

Method

1 Measure the length and width of the pastel to be framed, in this example 55 × 37 in (139 × 93 cm). To cut the plywood, add ¾ in (18 mm) to these dimensions on all sides, for overlapping the back of the frame. The balsa mouldings, which will secure the glass in the frame, should be as deep as the frame rebate when the glass is in position. The glass, ¹/₁₀ in (3 mm) thick, should be cut to the dimensions of the pastel.

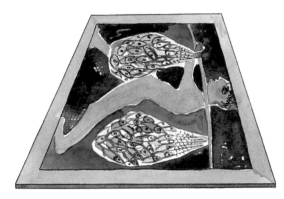

To fix the plywood backing to the pastel, refer to page 78, step 2.

𝒯𝒾𝓅
Use a large work surface!

2 Very gently place the plywood with the pastel face down on the work surface. Using the bradawl, make holes through the plywood every 2 in (5 cm), ¼ in (6 mm) from the edge.

3 Position the glass in the frame, then stick the balsa mouldings against the rebate, following steps 5 to 8 on pages 79–80.

4 *Place the plywood with the pastel so that it sits over the back of the frame moulding, overlapping it by ¾ in (18 mm) all round. Gently hollow out the holes pierced in the plywood using the bradawl.*

𝒯 𝒾 𝓅

For greater security, cut four triangular pieces of ⅙-in (4-mm) thick mountboard or hardboard, large enough to hold the plywood in place. Apply glue to one surface of each triangle and stick them over each corner of the frame. Nail down with small nails.

7 *Hang the picture on the wall from a cord tied between the two eyes.*

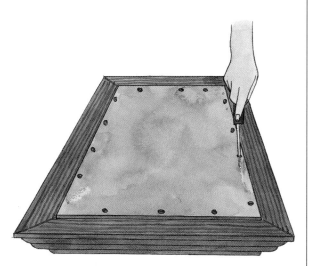

5 *Secure the backing board to the frame by screwing small screws down through the holes. Do not use nails as the vibrations could disturb the pastel.*

6 *On one side of the back of the frame, make a hole with the bradawl 10 in (25 cm) from the top. Screw an eye into the hole until firmly in place. Repeat for the other side of the frame.*

An interesting way of bringing together several subjects of the same genre is to frame them individually and then put them all into one large frame. This method is especially suitable for showing off antique engravings, family photos or prints of fruit or flowers. The frames can also include decorated or bevelled mounts. Any style of frame can be used, chosen according to the type of subject or where you plan to hang it.

FRAMES WITHIN FRAMES

MATERIALS

Frame saw	Paintbrush
1½-in (4-cm) wide	Backing board
moulding	Cutter
Metal scale rule	Heavy ruler
HB or H pencil	30 metal fixing plates
Gesso	Nails
Paint and red pigment	Hammer
Red and orange paints	Pliers

MULTIPLE FRAMES

This example uses a ready-made large frame big enough to contain nine smaller frames, three across and three down. All the frames are painted. Start by measuring the width of the moulding of the large frame and choose the small frame mouldings to complement this. For instance, if your large frame moulding is 3½ in (9 cm) wide, choose mouldings 1½ in (4 cm) wide for the smaller frames. The use of a frame saw is strongly recommended.

Measuring the moulding of the small frames

1 Place the large frame face down on the work surface. Measure the height of the opening with the ruler against the rebate; in this case it is 38 in (97 cm). Repeat for the width, which in this example is 30 in (78 cm).

2 Add the number of vertical mouldings for the small frames which will be placed across the larger frame, in this case six. To calculate the space occupied by the mouldings, multiply this figure by the width of the moulding – 1½ in (4 cm) – giving 9 in (23 cm).

3 To calculate the total height of the pictures within the smaller frames when set in the large frame, deduct 9 in (23 cm) from 38 in (97 cm) to give 29 in (74 cm).

4 Divide this amount by three (the number of small frames) to obtain the height of one small picture: 9⅔ in (24.6 cm).

5 To calculate the width of each small picture, use the same method:
6 × 1½ in (4 cm) = 9 in (23 cm), 30 – 9 = 21 in (78 – 23 = 55 cm);
21 ÷ 3 = 7 in (55 ÷ 3 = 17.5 cm) wide.
The dimensions of each small frame are therefore 9⅔ × 7 in (24.6 × 17.5 cm).

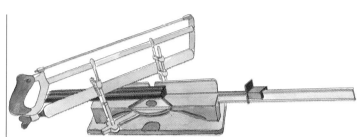

Cutting the mouldings

Start by cutting the long sides of the small frame mouldings.

1 *Place the length of moulding on the work surface and measure 9⅔ in (24.6 cm).*

2 *Position the blade of the saw to cut the first angle, on the left. Place the lip side of the moulding against the plate of the saw, allowing the left-hand end of the moulding to extend slightly beyond the saw. Gently lower the saw on to the moulding and cut the angle.*

3 *Position the blade of the saw at the specific point for cutting the moulding to the right length. Start by cutting a 90° angle before making the angled cut. Replace the moulding with the lip side against the saw plate with the cut angle on the left. Ensure that the cut mark is perfectly aligned with the blade. Cut the right-hand angle. Remove the blade of the saw from this side.*

Tip

To make sure that the mark is perfectly aligned with the blade of the saw, bend down so that you are at eye level with the saw, holding it with your right hand. Lower it towards the mark without letting the blade touch the moulding, and ensure that the blade is in line with the start of the mark. The frame saw has a stop, which allows you to cut any number of mouldings to the same length as the first, without having to remeasure every time.

4 Position the stop on the left-hand side of the saw in the position provided. Gently lower the blade and let it rest on the support. Take the cut length of moulding and place its right-hand angle against the blade (the lip side still against the saw plate). Slide the stop up against the left-hand angle and fix it in place. This will give you the measurement for all the pieces of the same length.

5 Repeat 18 times to obtain 18 mouldings of identical size.

6 For the shorter sides, repeat 18 times using the appropriate measurement, in this example 7 in (17.5 cm).

7 To assemble the frames, see 'Simple picture framing: Measuring, cutting and assembling the moulding' on pages 28–9, steps 8 to 14.

Painting the frames

If the large frame is old, you can give it a coat of gesso (see page 17) for a smooth finish before painting it in your chosen colour. Paint the smaller frames in complementary colours. Any colours are possible, but your choice should depend on the décor of the room in which the ensemble will be hung.

1 Apply one or two coats of gesso to the main frame and leave to dry for an hour.

2 Add a little red pigment to the red paint and mix. Apply to the whole of the frame with the paintbrush, starting with one of the longer sides.

3 Apply the red or orange paint directly to the smaller frames. Several coats may be needed.

Tip

It's possible to vary the red shades of the smaller frames to make them darker or lighter. Apply several coats for a darker shade and a coat of white underneath for a lighter shade.

4 Put the frames on one side to dry.

Measuring and cutting the backing board

1 Transfer the internal dimensions of one of the smaller frames to a piece of backing board with a pencil and ruler. Join the marks.

2 Cut the card along the lines using the heavy ruler and cutter.

3 Cut eight more pieces of backing board in the same way.

If the pictures are smaller than the frames, make a mount with or without a bevelled window. Refer to 'Framing with a mount' on page 32 or 'Framing with a bevelled window mount' on page 42, following the step-by-step instructions.

Tip

Vary the size of the mount depending on the subject to be framed, for a highly original effect.

Final assembly

To assemble the small frames, see 'Simple picture framing: final assembly' on pages 30–31.

1 Place three smaller frames face down on the work surface. Arrange them side by side horizontally.

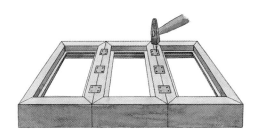

2 Take three metal plates and position them over the gap between the first and second frames. The first plate should be 1½ in (4 cm) from the top of the frame, the third 1½ in (4 cm) from the bottom, and the second between the two. Nail them in place with the hammer, tapping the nails gently through the holes provided.

3 Repeat step 2 to fix the second frame to the third.

Tip

Before fixing the small frames together, place them face up on the work surface and decide on their final arrangement.

4 Place the next three small frames face down on the work surface and join them together as before.

5 Repeat for the last three frames.

6 Place two rows of small frames one below the other. Take two metal plates and place them over the gap between the first two frames in the top and second row. Nail them in place using the holes provided, tapping the nails in gently with the hammer. Fix the two rows together in this way.

7 *Place the third row below the second, and follow step 6 to fix the metal plates in place.*

8 *Place the large frame face down on the work surface. Place the arrangement of smaller frames inside it.*

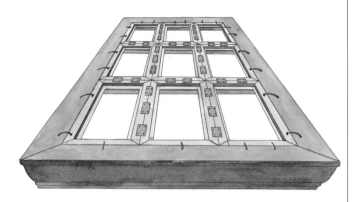

9 *To complete the assembly, drive long nails into the back of the outer frame moulding at 4-in (10-cm) intervals. Using pliers, fold them down at right angles over the back of the inner frames, tapping them down gently with a hammer.*

Disparate subjects

This method involves framing several different kinds of picture in the same style within one large frame. You can achieve an interesting effect by putting together pictures of different sizes or styles in a single frame, either in pairs or an odd number. To help you decide how disparate items will look together, try out the arrangements beforehand on a sheet of paper. This will also help you decide whether to give them a decorative mount, with or without a bevelled edge, and to consider the best type of moulding to use for the outer and inner frames.

The example below consists of five items of similar size. One is placed in the centre of the big frame, within a large mount taller than it is wide. The other four are in smaller mounts and frames of the same size, in pairs on each side of the central picture. This project is assembled as described in the preceding section, 'Multiple frames' on pages 84–8.

PANEL FRAME

This type of frame is a stylish way of setting off a canvas, stucco pieces, wood sculptures and many other kinds of decorative item. This panel frame has two parts, a top part containing a decorative element and a lower part containing a mirror. If you are using a canvas for the top section, give it a fine, plain frame moulding beforehand, to prevent damage when you fit it to the panel frame. A moulding will conceal the join between the two sections.

A panel frame is not usually hung, but placed on a piece of furniture, mantelpiece or side table. A classic panel frame has an outer decorative moulding at least 2 in (5 cm) wide, and the inner mouldings around the two elements should be of a similar style. The inner and outer mouldings may be painted. If the outer moulding is bought ready-painted, the inner moulding should be painted in a matching or complementary colour.

You can give a panel frame a modern look, as in the example shown here. The decorative element is a modern painting and the inner frames are made from plain 1½-in (4-cm) moulding. The outer frame surrounding the whole is made from a modern frame moulding, wide, simple and lightly painted. The colours you choose are up to you. You could opt for unity, or play on the idea of complementing the colours in your picture, picking out one for the inner frames and another for the outer frame.

MATERIALS

Backing board	Sponge
Modern painting	Cloth
Mirror	Fine glasspaper
1½-in (4-cm) wide flat	2¾-in (7-cm) nails
moulding	Paints in colours to
Wide, plain modern	complement the painting
moulding	Pliers
Wood glue	5 metallic fixing plates
Cord clamp	Hammer

Method

The first step is to make the frames for the picture and the mirror with the 1½-in (4-cm) moulding. Next, make the outer frame, and finally assemble all the elements.

Making the painting frame

1 *Measure the painting, which in this case is 23 in (59 cm) wide by 15 in (38 cm) high.*

2 *Cut the frame mouldings to these dimensions and assemble them as explained in the section 'Simple picture framing: Measuring cutting and assembling the moulding' on pages 27–9.*

3 *Sand the cut edges with glasspaper, apply wood glue and assemble the mouldings in the cord clamp.*

4 *After the required setting time, take off the clamp and remove any excess glue with a damp sponge and cloth.*

5 *Sand the top, back and corners of the frame until the wood is smooth.*

6 *Place the frame face up on the work surface, one edge overhanging slightly. Paint this side of the frame from the lip towards the back. Turn it round to paint the other three sides in the same way. Apply two or three coats and leave to dry.*

7 *Insert the painting in the frame. Hammer long nails in ½ in (12 mm) deep all around the frame at 3-in (7.5-cm) intervals. Bend them at right angles using the pliers, so that they hold down the back of the stretcher of the painting.*

Making the mirror frame

1 *The mirror should be the same width as the painting, in this example 23 × 27½ in (59 × 70 cm). Have it cut to these dimensions.*

2 *Cut the mouldings to the dimensions of the mirror and assemble the frame as explained above.*

3 *Paint the frame in the same colour as the frame of the painting.*

4 *Cut a piece of backing board the same size as the mirror.*

5 *With the frame face down on the work surface, install the mirror and the backing board into the frame.*

6 *At each angle of the frame, insert two nails (one on each side of the corner) into the moulding rebate, across the backing board.*

Making the outer frame

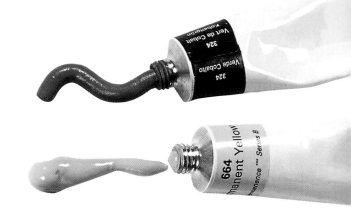

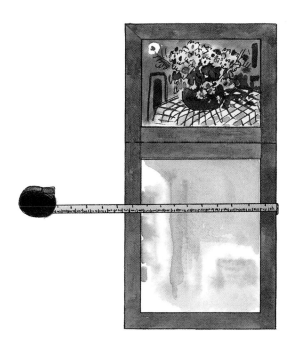

1 Place the framed picture and mirror face down and in position, one below the other, on the work surface. Measure the total width and height of these two elements with a tape measure, in this case 23 × 42½ in (59 × 118 cm).

2 To obtain the dimensions of the outer frame, add ¹⁄₁₂ in (2 mm) play to these dimensions: 23¹⁄₁₂ × 42⁷⁄₁₂ (59.2 × 118.2 cm).

3 Cut and assemble the outer frame as explained above.

4 Paint the frame in your chosen colour; in this example it will be green.

Joining the painting frame to the mirror frame

1 Place the painting frame and the mirror frame face down on the work surface, one below the other.

2 Position five metal plates over the gap between the two frames. Fix the first and fifth plate 1½ in (4 cm) from the edges of the frames, and the other three evenly spaced between them.

3 Nail them in place, tapping the nails gently through the holes provided with the hammer.

Final assembly

1 Place the outer panel frame face down on the work surface and insert the two joined frames into it.

2 To fix all the elements together, hammer nails into the back of the outer frame at 4-in (10-cm) intervals. Using pliers, fold them down at right angles over the back of the inner frames. Tap them down gently with a hammer.

Lines and washes have been used as borders for pictures since antiquity: the frescoes and mosaics that decorated luxury homes in Roman times would have been edged with wide borders and decorative motifs. Lines and washes require top-quality pens and inks, and are best done on mountboard specially finished to take washes. This type of mount looks best with a bevelled edge.

LINES AND WASHES

MATERIALS

Mountboard	Eraser
Heavy ruler	Cutter
Metal scale rule	Paper knife
Metal set square	Very fine glasspaper
HB or H pencil	Syringe or dropper
Rotring pen	Cup
Rotring ink	Raphael 803 No. 2
Blue ink	paintbrush
Gilded paper	PVA adhesive

THE CLASSIC LINE AND WASH

The classic line and wash border has one or more bands of colour on a light background, a band of gilding and several fine ink lines, called fillets. For a wide border in this style, it's best to have a number of lines set close together round the edges of the window, for a harmonious overall effect. Always use a template when applying a line and wash.

Traditionally, fillets were drawn in brown ink, and a band of gilding was applied between the second and third lines out from the window. Don't use self-adhesive strips of gilding, as these peel away with age. The inks come in various colours, and are diluted with water. If you mix your own ink colours, use a syringe or dropper and note how many drops you use to create each shade. Test them out on an offcut of mountboard. Don't store mixed colours for long because they will change colour as they evaporate. Before applying a line and wash, always make a template of your design, cut from mountboard.

Measuring and cutting the mount

Once you have measured the subject to be framed (as explained in 'Framing with a mount' on page 32), decide on the width of the mount margins. For a mount with a wash the margin should be the same width all round, and the corners of the window absolutely square.

1 Measure the width and height of your picture, which in this example is 12×16 in (30×40 cm). Deduct $\frac{1}{10}$ in (3 mm) from each side (to be covered by the mount) to obtain the dimensions of the window: here $11\frac{4}{5} \times 15\frac{4}{5}$ in (29.4×39.4 cm).

2 Add the margins of the mount to these measurements to obtain the outer dimensions of the mount.
$11\frac{4}{5} + 3\frac{1}{4} + 3\frac{1}{4}$ in $= 18\frac{3}{10}$ in ($29.4 + 8 + 8$ cm $= 45.4$ cm) high
$15\frac{4}{5} + 3\frac{1}{4} + 3\frac{1}{4}$ in $= 22\frac{3}{10}$ in ($39.4 + 8 + 8$ cm $= 55.4$ cm) wide
Cut out the mount to these measurements, which are also used for the backing board.

3 With the scale rule and sharp pencil, mark the dimensions of the mount window on the mount, placed face down on the work surface. Without pressing, lightly join the marks, crossing them over slightly at the corners.

4 Mark each corner by digging in slightly with the cutter. Position the ruler on each of the pencil lines in turn and cut from one end to the other, making sure that the cutter does not run over the corners.

5 Remove the centre of the mount to form the window, and lightly sand the inside edges with very fine glasspaper, ensuring that you do not damage the edges or the corners.

Making the template

Choose the style of border you require and then make up the template as follows.

1 *Cut a rectangle of mountboard 3¼ in (8 cm) wide (the width of the margin of the mount) and 6 in (15 cm) long.*

2 *Mark with pencil dots, at each end of the template, the spacings chosen for the fillets and bands of wash. In this example the lines are ¼ in (6 mm) from the edge, then ¹⁄₁₀ in from this first line, then ⅛ in, ¹⁄₁₀ in, ¾ in and ¼ in (6 mm, 3 mm, 4 mm, 3 mm, 18 mm, 5 mm).*

3 *Before using, practise drawing lines with the Rotring pen on an offcut of mountboard.*

4 *Join the marks, inclining the pen to a greater or lesser extent to vary the thickness of the lines, which will give a relief effect to the wash.*

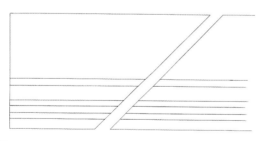

5 *Cut the template at a 45° angle, using the metal set square.*

Applying the lines and wash to the mount

The ink fillets

1 *Place the mount face up on the work surface. With a fine pencil and very light pressure, draw the four diagonals at the corners.*

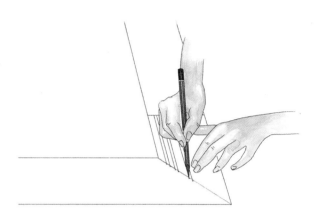

2 *Place the marked template on one of these diagonals with the shorter edge against the window opening and the diagonal cut edge along the diagonal of the corner. Transfer the marks of the lines on the template to the mount with a fine pencil, using the lightest pressure.*

3 *Repeat at the other three corners. Join up these marks with a pencil, completing one rectangle at a time.*

4 Using the plain side of the ruler (without the scale), draw in the ink fillets, starting from the first mark and finishing a fraction before the next to make sure it does not overrun. Continue with the same line around the mount to complete each rectangle, always finishing the line just a fraction from the end. It is important to complete each rectangle before moving on to the next, so that you can vary the width of the lines to create rectangles with different line thicknesses. The lines bordering the colour wash should not be drawn in ink.

Tip

Test the pen on an offcut of mountboard before each application, to prevent blots. You can go over a line with the pen more than once.

5 Allow the lines to dry thoroughly before removing the pencil lines. Rub them out very gently with the eraser.

Tip

Allow about 20 minutes for the lines to dry.

The colour wash
Choose a shade that complements both the picture and the décor of the room.

1 To mix your colour, use a cup and a syringe or dropper. Take two teaspoons (10 ml) of water and add two drops of the desired colour (blue in this example). Test the shade on an offcut of mountboard. To lighten the shade, add water drop by drop; to darken it, add more drops of ink.

2 Pass the paintbrush, slightly moistened with water, over the band to be coloured, to remove traces of dressing from the mountboard.

Tip

Since this operation requires a lot of care, practise moistening the brush and passing it over some mountboard before starting on your actual piece of work.

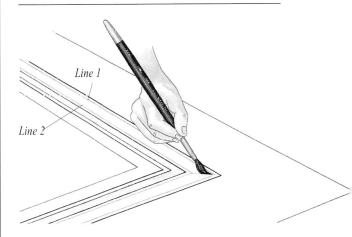

Line 1

Line 2

3 When you are sure that you have removed all traces of shine from the area to be coloured and let it dry, dip the brush in the coloured ink. Since painting the wash is delicate work, follow these instructions carefully:
• *Place a drop of ink from the brush in corner A.*
• *Draw the drop from corner A to corner B. Lift the brush.*
• *Reposition the brush, pressing it down lightly until the bristles cover the whole width of the band between lines 1 and 2.*
• *Holding it vertical, draw the brush fairly quickly but evenly down the band to the next corner of the mount.*
• *Reposition the brush on the next corner and repeat the procedure. Do the same for the other two sides.*
• *Rinse and shake out the brush. Use the tip to remove any last drops of ink to prevent cloudy patches forming.*

Tip

If the wash has darker blotches here and there, you can even them out by passing the brush, lightly moistened with water, over them, but this has to be done very quickly.

Applying the gilded paper

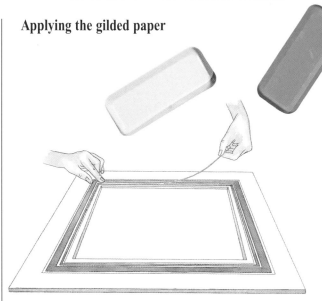

4 *Place the mount to one side and leave to dry.*

5 *Draw ink borders around the edges of the colour wash.*

1 *Place a piece of gilded paper face down on a sheet of glass or steel, and cut several strips $\frac{1}{10}$ in (3 mm) wide.*

2 *Brush adhesive on to the back of one of the strips. To position it on the mount, hold one end with the fingertips and guide it into place between the lines that will border it, letting it overrun the corners slightly. Gently press into place with the paper knife. With the cutter and heavy ruler, cut both ends of the fillet to size where they overlap the corners.*

3 *Repeat for the other three sides and leave to dry.*

4 *Once everything is thoroughly dry, attach the picture as described on page 35, steps 1 to 5, and assemble the frame as described in 'Simple picture framing' on pages 24–31.*

Tip

Since line and wash borders demand delicacy and skill, it is vital to have plenty of practice before you make the final mount.

ANTIQUE-STYLE WASHES

Traditionally, antique-style washes have two or more bands of colour across the whole mount. From the window edge, an uncoloured border is followed by a band of light colour, and then a narrow uncoloured band might be followed by a band of gilding. Another narrow uncoloured border is followed by a third band of colour deeper than the first, which usually borders on a final margin of an even deeper colour, extending to the outer edge of the mount.

MATERIALS

Mountboard	Eraser
Heavy ruler	Cutter
Metal scale rule	Paper knife
Metal set square	Very fine glasspaper
Gilded paper	Syringe or dropper
HB or H pencil	Cup
Rotring pen	Raphael 803 No. 2
Brown Rotring ink	paintbrush
Yellow, green and	
turquoise ink	

Applying the wash to the mount

1 *Decide on the dimensions of the mount margins, which in this example are 3½ in (9 cm) wide. Make up the mount (see pages 92–3), ensuring that the corners of the window are perfect right angles.*

2 *Make up the template from a rectangle of mountboard 3½ in (9 cm) wide and 6 in (15 cm) long. Mark in pencil the widths chosen for the bands, at the top and bottom of the template, for example: ¼ in (6 mm) from the edge of the window, then ¼ in (6 mm), ¹⁄₁₂ in (2 mm), ⅓ in (8 mm), ¹⁄₁₂ in (2 mm), ⅓ in (8 mm), ¹⁄₁₀ in (3 mm), ½ in (12 mm) and so on.*

3 *Join the marks, inclining the pen to a greater or lesser extent to vary the widths of the lines and give a relief effect to the washes.*

4 *Cut the template at a 45° angle, using the set square.*

8 Pass the brush, slightly moistened with water, over the band to be coloured, to remove all traces of dressing from the mountboard. Leave to dry thoroughly. Apply a band of coloured ink as described on page 95.

9 Once the first band is thoroughly dry, colour the other bands in the same way, to the outer edge of the mount, Once the first coats are completely dry, you can apply a second for a deeper colour.

10 Allow the colour wash bands to dry. Finish by applying the gilded paper, as described on page 96.

5 Place the mount face up on the work surface. With a fine pencil, very lightly draw in the diagonal line at each corner.

6 Place the marked template on one diagonal, lining it up with the edge of the window and the diagonal line on the mount. With a sharp pencil, very lightly transfer the marks on the template to the mount. Repeat for the other three corners. Join all the points with light pencil lines.

7 Place a dessertspoonful of water in a cup. Using a syringe or dropper, add three drops of yellow, two of green and one of turquoise ink.

11 With the pen, draw in the ink lines over the pencil lines, completing each rectangle before moving on to the next. Finish each line a fraction before the corners so that it does not overrun. Vary the thickness of each line for different rectangles, referring to your template.

12 Allow to dry before very gently erasing the pencil marks.

13 Attach the picture to the mount (see page 35), and assemble the frame as described in the section 'Simple picture framing' on pages 24–31.

OCTAGONAL LINES AND WASHES

An octagonal line and wash surround is a very stylish way of showing off an antique print. Because of the strong shape, keep the wash quite light so that it does not overpower the picture. The angles of a mount of this kind must be perfectly true.

You apply the lines and wash in the same way as for the other projects in this section. The only difference is in the template, which will not have a 45° angle. You will have to trace one of the octagonal corners direct from the mount when making the template which, this time, is made from thick tracing paper.

Giving an octagonal window a bevelled edge will make it look even more elegant.

MATERIALS

Mountboard	Eraser
Tracing paper	Cutter
Weight	Paper knife
Heavy ruler	Very fine glasspaper
Metal scale rule	Syringe or dropper
HB or H pencil	Cup
Rotring pen	Raphael 803 No. 2
Brown Rotring ink	paintbrush
Yellow ink	

Measuring and cutting the bevelled mount

1 *Measure the picture and decide on the width of the mount margins, which should all be equal: in this case 4 in (10 cm).*

2 *To make the bevels, see 'Framing with an octagonal bevelled mount' on pages 55–7, and follow the step-by-step instructions.*

Making the template

1 *Cut a piece of thick tracing paper 4 in (10 cm) wide and 6 in (15 cm) long.*

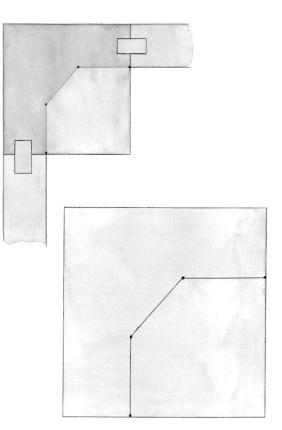

2 *Position the tracing paper over one of the corners of the mount and trace the lines of the window angles.*

Tip

Use quite a large piece of tracing paper and make sure that one corner is a perfect right angle. Position this right angle so it just slightly overlaps the edge of the mount. Weight it in place so that it doesn't slip when you trace the lines of the corner.

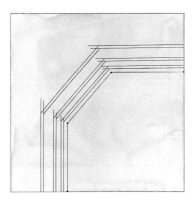

3 *In pencil, mark round the two octagonal angles the points where you want the spacing of the lines and washes.*

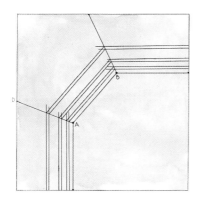

4 *Join up the marks on the template very precisely, using the pen.*

5 *Check that the angles are correct, and cut the template using the cutter and heavy ruler.*

Applying the line and wash to the mount

The ink fillets

Refer to page 94 and follow the step-by-step instructions.

Transfer the marks so that you will be able to draw the lines all round the octagon, positioning the template over each corner in turn.

The colour wash

In this example, the band of colour wash is yellow.

To fill in the wash, follow the step-by-step instructions on page 95.

The final assembly is as for the other frames with a line-and-wash mount described in this section.

Fancy line-and-wash effects allow you to add an original, personal touch to a mount. All kinds of ornamental flourishes can be added, including circles, geometric patterns, intertwined windows, marbling, garlands, bows, flowers and foliage.
You can also stick dried flowers and leaves or other pretty objects to a colour-wash border.

FANCY LINE-AND-WASH EFFECTS

MATERIALS

Mountboard	Eraser
Tracing paper	Cutter
Weight	Very fine glasspaper
Heavy ruler	Dropper
Metal scale rule	Cup
Metal set square	Raphael 803 No. 2
HB and 2B pencils	paintbrush
Rotring pen	Isabey 6232 No. 3
Black Rotring ink	paintbrush
Blue and yellow ink	

BOWS

For this project, the bow design, which you can draw freehand or copy from an original, is transferred to the mount with tracing paper. The colours used here are red and blue; the fillets are black.

Measuring and cutting the mount

Decide on the width of the margins of the mount for the subject to be framed, making them all the same. As for all mounts, make the corners of the window perfectly square.

1 *Measure the subject to be framed, which in this example is 9½ × 14½ in (24.3 × 37 cm). Deduct ¹⁄₁₀ in (3 mm) from each side (to be covered by the mount) to obtain the dimensions of the window: here 9³⁄₁₀ × 14³⁄₁₀ in (23.7 × 36.4 cm).*

2 *To these measurements add the width of the mount, in our example 3 in (7.5 cm). This will give you the outer dimensions of the mount as well as the backing board.*
9³⁄₁₀ + 3 + 3 in = 15³⁄₁₀ in (23.7 + 7.5 + 7.5 cm = 38.7 cm) high
14³⁄₁₀ + 3 + 3 in = 20³⁄₁₀ in (36.4 + 7.5 + 7.5 cm = 51.9 cm) wide.

3 *Cut out the mount to the required dimensions from a piece of mountboard placed face down on the work surface.*

4 *Use the ruler to mark the dimensions of the mount window using a sharp*

pencil. Without pressing, lightly join the
marks, crossing them over slightly at the
corners.

5 Mark each corner by digging in slightly
with the cutter. Position the heavy ruler on
each of the pencil lines in turn and cut from
one end to the other, making sure that the
cutter does not overrun where the lines
intersect.

6 Remove the centre of the mount and lightly
sand the inner edges with very fine
glasspaper, ensuring that you don't damage the
edges or corners.

Making the template

1 Cut a rectangle of mountboard 3 in (7.5 cm)
wide and 6 in (15 cm) long.

2 Mark with pencil dots, on the top and bottom
of the template, the dimensions chosen for the
spacing of the ink lines and bands of colour
wash.

3 Take the Rotring pen and test it. Join the
marks on the template with the pen.

4 Cut the template, having drawn on a 45°
angle with the set square.

Applying the line and wash to the mount

The ink fillets

1 *Place the mount face up on the work surface. With a fine pencil and very light pressure, mark the diagonal at each corner. Don't try to erase these pencil lines before the ink has dried thoroughly, or it will smudge.*

2 *Place the marked template on one of these diagonals, lining up the shorter edge against the window and the diagonal cut along the diagonal of the corner. Transfer the positions of the lines on the template to the mount with a fine pencil, using the lightest pressure.*

3 *Repeat at the other three corners.*

4 *Place the plain side of the ruler (without the scale) between two reference marks of the same level and draw in the ink lines, starting from the first mark and finishing a fraction before the next to make sure it does not overrun. Continue with the same line around the remaining borders to complete a rectangle. It is important to complete each rectangle before moving on to the next, and to let the ink dry thoroughly before starting the next line, to avoid smudging. If necessary, touch in any gaps near the reference marks by hand, without the ruler.*

5 *Remove the pencil lines by rubbing very gently with a spotlessly clean eraser.*

The bows

Choose bows of the right proportions for the frame and the line-and-wash design. One goes in each corner outside the fillets. They will be the same colour as the outer band of wash (the one farthest away from the window), and drawn very finely in ink so that they don't overshadow the subject.

1 *Draw a bow of suitable size on tracing paper, or choose one from a book or magazine and trace it. With a soft pencil (2B), blacken the back of the tracing paper over the back of the lines of the bow.*

2 *Centre the motif diagonally across one corner. Weight down the edges of the tracing paper to stop it moving while you trace the design.*

3 *Lightly trace the design onto the mount with a fine, sharp pencil. Remove the tracing paper and check that the image is complete.*

4 *Repeat for the other three bows.*

5 Draw over the pencil lines in ink, without pressing too hard. Let each bow dry thoroughly before moving on to the next.

6 Once the ink of the bows has dried, lightly rub out the pencil lines with a spotlessly clean eraser.

Colouring the bands of wash and bows

Choose shades that complement the picture, and also the décor of the room where it will be hung. For this type of fancy wash you can use the same colour for the motif and the ink fillets. In the example pictured on page 103, these are yellow, and the broad band of wash is light blue.

1 For the blue wash, put a tablespoon (15 ml) of water into a cup using a syringe or dropper. Add two drops of blue ink. Test the shade on an offcut of mountboard and add more water or ink if necessary, depending on the desired effect.

2 Dampen the brush with water and pass it lightly over the section of mountboard to be coloured, to remove all traces of dressing. Leave to dry.

3 Apply the wash to the band as described on page 95.

4 Put the mount to one side and leave to dry.

5 Put a tablespoon of water (15 ml) into a cup. Add four drops of yellow ink. Test the shade on an offcut of mountboard, and if necessary add more water or ink to lighten or darken the shade.

6 To colour the bows, use the finer brush, checking that it is the right width on an offcut of card.

7 Dampen the brush with water and pass it lightly over each bow.

8 Apply the colour wash to each bow, starting with the top left-hand one. It is important to colour one at a time to avoid smudging.

9 Colour the other three bows in the same way.

10 Put the mount to one side to dry. Attach the picture to the mount (see page 35) and then assemble the frame, following the instructions in 'Simple picture framing: Final assembly' on pages 30–31.

CIRCLES

The washes on this mount are in green and yellow ink, highlighted by a bevelled edge painted green. You will need a template to draw the circles.

MATERIALS

Mountboard	Brown Rotring ink
Bevelling board	Green and yellow ink
Heavy ruler	Eraser
Metal scale rule	Cutter
Metal set square	Very fine glasspaper
Circle template	Dropper
HB or H pencil	Cup
Green paint	Raphael 803 No. 2
Rotring pen	paintbrush

Measuring and cutting the mounts

This project includes both a top mount and a bevelled mount. The backing board measures 26 × 22 in (67.2 × 55.4 cm); the subject 7¹/₁₂ × 9½ in (18.2 × 24.1 cm); the bevelled edge ¼ in (6 mm); and the top mount margins 4 in (10 cm).
Make the top mount as described in 'Bows' on page 102. For the bevelled window mount, refer to 'Bevelling' on page 42. The margins of the mount should all be the same width.

Making the template

1 Cut a rectangle of mountboard 4 in (10 cm) wide and 6 in (15 cm) long.

2 Mark with pencil dots, on the top and bottom of this template, the distance between the fillets, including a band ⅘ in (20 mm) wide for the circles.

3 Carefully join up the marks on the template with the pen.

4 Within the ⅘-in (20-mm) band, draw circles of appropriate diameter using the circle template.

5 Draw a 45° angle on the marked template, using the set square. Cut the angle with the cutter.

Applying the wash to the mount

The ink fillets

1 With the mount face up on the work surface, very lightly mark the diagonal at each corner.

2 Place the marked template on one of these diagonals, lining up the shorter edge against the window and the diagonal edge with the diagonal line at the corner. Transfer the marks of the lines on the template to the mount with a fine pencil, using the lightest pressure.

3 Repeat the procedure for the other three corners. Place the plain side of the ruler (without the scale) between the reference marks at the same level and join them up with a pencil.

4 Draw in the ink fillets. Run the pen from the first mark, finishing a fraction before the next to make sure it does not overrun. Continue with the same line around the remaining borders to complete a rectangle. Allow each line to dry thoroughly before starting the next, to avoid smudging. It is important to complete each rectangle before starting the next.

5 Do not ink in the lines bordering the band that will contain the circles. Allow the ink to dry thoroughly before gently rubbing out the pencil lines.

6 Position the circle template in the centre of the band. Using a pencil, draw circles right round the band, moving the template as appropriate.

Tip

Before drawing the circles, check that they will all fit neatly within the space given. If they do not, you can adjust the gaps between the circles slightly in the middle or at the corners.

The colour wash

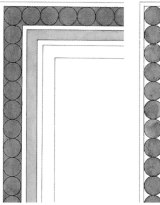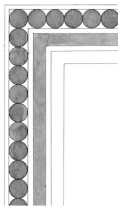

A FLOWERY BORDER

Unlike other colour wash techniques, here only the circles themselves are coloured, giving an amazing effect. Use quite a fine brush, and take great care; this is very delicate work. If you are not sure of yourself, you can colour the whole band and draw in the circles with ink.

1 *Put a tablespoon (15 ml) of water in a cup and add three drops of ink in the chosen colour. Test the shade on an offcut of mountboard. If necessary, add more water or ink to achieve the desired effect.*

2 *Dampen the brush slightly and pass it over the band, to remove all traces of dressing from the mountboard. Leave to dry.*

3 *With the brush, apply a drop of ink to the centre of a circle, and spread it gently over the whole circle. Colour each circle separately.*

4 *Put the mount to one side and leave to dry for an hour.*

5 *Take the circle template and draw in the circumference of each circle with the pen. Don't rub out the pencil lines, as this could affect the colour.*

This style of mountboard decoration is done in the same way as the other types of line-and-wash borders, but with the addition of flowers. These can be tiny dried flowers or flower petals, or photos or drawings of flowers cut from old magazines or flower catalogues. They can be stuck on an uncoloured section of the mount or on a band of colour wash.

In order to ensure a balanced overall effect, the mount margins should be about 4 in (10 cm) wide.

MATERIALS

Mountboard	PVA adhesive
Dried flowers	Eraser
Heavy ruler	Cutter
Metal scale rule	Very fine glasspaper
Metal set square	Dropper
HB or H pencil	Cup
Rotring pen	Raphael 803 No. 2
Brown Rotring ink	paintbrush
Coloured ink	

Making the template

Start by taking the largest flower, and add ¼ in (6 mm) to its diameter to obtain the width of the colour wash band, leaving a space on each side between the flower and the ink fillet.
To make the template, refer to the preceding section.

Applying the line and wash and flowers

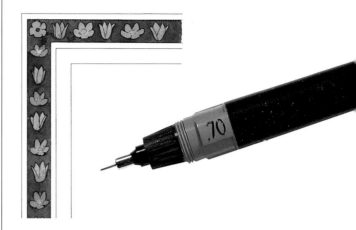

Refer to the section 'Circles' on page 106 for applying all the elements of the line and wash. If you want to paint the flower border, see the instructions in 'The classic line and wash' on pages 92–5.

Making the mount

1 *Calculate the width of the mount on the basis of the chosen width of the flower band and the spacing between the lines. There should also be a reasonable space between the last line and the outer edge of the mount.*

2 *Refer to the section 'Framing with a mount' on pages 32–4, and make up the mount following the step-by-step instructions.*

Tip

Dry flower petals or small flowers by pressing them between two sheets of tissue or blotting paper inserted in the leaves of a book and weighted down for several days. Choose brightly coloured flowers as the colours fade slightly as they dry.

1 *Take your petals, dried flowers or cut-out flowers. With a brush, apply a dot of PVA adhesive to each one in turn and stick them evenly round the whole band.*

2 *Place a clean piece of backing board over the mount and press for two hours.*

3 *Once the mount is pressed and complete, attach the picture (see page 35) and carry out the final assembly, referring to the section 'Simple picture framing: Final assembly' on pages 30–31.*

MARBLED BORDERS

Instead of applying a plain wash of colour to a mount, you can create a band of marbling. To obtain clean edges, place a strip of adhesive paper on each side of the band to be marbled. Buy this paper from a specialist picture-framing supplier, as certain types of adhesive paper may spoil the surface of the mount, or allow colour to seep through. It's best to add the ink lines with the pen once the marbled band is finished and dry.

In this example, the marbled band is blue-grey and may be given yellow fillets with a hint of pink.

MATERIALS

Mountboard	Blue (light, medium, dark),
Protective adhesive	brown and yellow inks
paper	Cutter
Heavy ruler	Very fine glasspaper
Metal scale rule	Sponge
Metal set square	Dropper
HB or H pencil	4 cups
Eraser	Raphael 803 No. 2
Rotring pen	paintbrush
Brown Rotring ink	Extra-fine paintbrush

Achieving a marbling effect

Choose your main colour, which you can dilute to different degrees in different cups. Use a second colour to add extra-fine lines to complete the marbled effect.

1 *Place a strip of protective adhesive paper on either side of the band to be painted.*

2 *Take three cups. Put four drops of water in one, plus one drop of light blue ink. Put one drop of water and two drops of dark blue ink in the second. Into the third cup, put one drop of water, two drops of brown ink and one drop of yellow to obtain an antique pink shade.*

3 *Brush a background of light blue ink over the band to be decorated.*

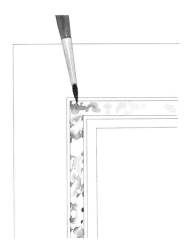

4 *Hold the brush by the end of the handle and paint fine wavy lines in dark blue. Rotate the brush between the thumb and the index finger to vary the thickness of the lines.*

Tip

It is important that the background colour is even. Never apply lines horizontally or vertically, always at an angle. You may go over some lines more than once to deepen the colour. To balance the effect, use a sponge dipped in the dark blue shade to fill in any gaps, completing the illusion. The choice of possible colours is very wide.

5 *Take the extra-fine brush and add some pinkish lines to fill out the effect. Finally, dip a brush in some ink and gently tap it above the marbling to add tiny splashes.*

6 *Put the mount to one side to dry for several hours. Gently remove the adhesive paper.*

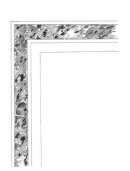

Tip

When you are happy with the finished effect, wait until the marbling is thoroughly dry before removing the adhesive paper.

7 *Draw in the ink fillets with the pen (refer to the section 'The ink fillets' on page 94).*

8 *Once the lines are thoroughly dry, attach the picture to the mount (see page 35) and assemble the frame as described in 'Simple picture framing' on pages 30–31.*

INTERLACED DESIGNS

This is a very pretty way of framing prints of fruits or animals, family photos, cherubs and other small groups of pictures. Choose items of the same size because the windows should be of the same format. The line and wash may be interlaced circles or squares surrounding square, diamond or circular windows. It's best not to add a bevelled edge to the windows of this kind of mount, as it already has plenty of detail.

MATERIALS

Plain mountboard	Coloured ink
Heavy ruler	Eraser
Metal scale rule	Cutter
Pair of compasses	Very fine glasspaper
HB or H pencil	Dropper
Coloured pencil (optional)	Cup
Rotring pen	Raphael 803 No. 2
Brown Rotring ink	paintbrush

Measuring and cutting the mount

1 *First, measure your pictures and decide on the size of the windows. In this example they are diamond-shaped. Make sure that the pictures are all the same size.*

2 *Make your calculations in the same way as for a single window mount. In the example shown, the windows are 3 × 3 in (7.5 × 7.5 cm). Add this dimension vertically between the windows, and twice this dimension horizontally – 6 in (15 cm) – and an 3-in (7.5-cm) margin around the whole mount.*

3 *Calculate all the dimensions of the mount. In this case the width is:*
3-in (7.5-cm) margin + 3-in (7.5-cm) window + 6-in (15-cm) space between + 3-in (7.5-cm) window + 3-in (7.5-cm) margin = 18 in (45 cm). The height of the mount will be 3 in (7.5 cm) less, that is, 15 in (37.5 cm).

4 *Transfer these measurements, 18 × 15 in (45 × 37.5 cm), to the mountboard and cut to size using the cutter and heavy ruler. Place the mountboard face up on the work surface. Draw a horizontal and vertical line bisecting it.*

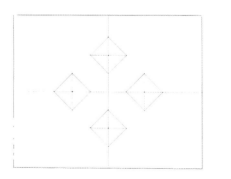

5 *Mark the centre of each diamond on the horizontal line 4½ in (12 cm) from the outer edges of the mount. Make a mark 1½ in (4 cm) on each side of the centres of the diamonds. Draw in the diamonds using the ruler and fine pencil. Repeat this step for the diamonds on the vertical axis.*

Applying the line and wash to the mount

The ink fillets

1 *Draw ink lines ¹⁄₁₀ and ¼ in (3 and 6 mm) from the windows. Allow to dry, and colour between the lines with coloured pencil if desired.*

2 *To make circles, place the point of the compasses at 3 in (7.5 cm) on the ruler scale and the lead at the 0 point, giving a diameter of 5 in (12.5 cm). Place the point in the centre of one of the diamonds and draw the first circle.*

3 *Draw a second circle 6 in (15 cm) in diameter. The ring formed by the two circles is the border for the wash. Add the rings around the three other diamond shapes.*

4 *To create the interlaced effect, gently erase the arcs of the circles which appear to pass beneath the others.*

5 *Draw over the outlines of the circles in ink and leave to dry thoroughly.*

The colour wash

Refer to 'The colour wash' on page 95–6 and follow steps 1 to 4 to colour in the rings.

Final assembly

1 *Place the mount on a sheet of glass and cut out the diamond-shaped windows using the cutter and heavy ruler, as described on page 34, steps 2 to 4.*

2 *Very gently erase all traces of pencil.*

3 *Attach the picture and assemble the frame as described in the previous section.*

You can use all types of moulding to make photo frames, and it's fun to personalise them in various ways. For example, you can cover them with a paper mosaic, stamps, old bank notes, buttons, shells, sweets, coloured ribbons or upholstery tacks. The backing board is not fixed permanently to the frame, but is easily removable to allow you to change the photos.

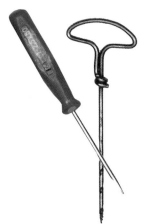

℘HOTO FRAMES

MATERIALS

Flat wooden	Newspaper
moulding	PVA adhesive
Bookbinding paper	Flat paintbrush
Mitre box	Paper knife
Saw	Glass
Metal scale rule	1 screw eye
Heavy ruler	4 clips
Backing board	Screwdriver
Cutter	Bradawl
Pencil	Clean cloth
Wood glue	Pair of scissors

A SIMPLE PHOTO FRAME

A simple frame may be made using various styles of moulding, with or without a personalised mount. This example is made from a simple wooden moulding covered with bookbinding paper. The moulding is covered before the frame is assembled. It is important to take the exact measurements of the photo you are framing, in order to make a frame to fit it perfectly.

First, measure the photo and cut out a backing board to the same dimensions. Cover one side of the backing board with bookbinding paper.

Measuring and cutting the moulding

Refer to 'Simple picture framing: Measuring, cutting and assembling the moulding' on pages 27–8, steps 1 to 8, but don't assemble the frame at this stage.

Decorating the frame moulding

1 *Take one of the cut pieces of moulding. Measure the base, the back, the top, the lip and the width of the rebate. Note these dimensions on a pad and add them together. Your total is the width to cut each strip of bookbinding paper.*

2 *Cut the lengths of bookbinding paper to the length of each moulding, plus 2½ in (6 cm) for each piece. Cut four strips to the correct width and length.*

Sticking the paper to the moulding is a delicate operation, which is why you must allow an extra amount for each side to ensure that the paper is not too short. Always start with the shorter sides. Check that there is no glue on the work surface or your hands.

3 *Place a strip of bookbinding paper face down on the work surface. Using the brush, apply adhesive to the base of the moulding.*

4 *Position the base of the moulding on the paper, with the interior face towards the cut side of the strip.*

5 *Turn over and gently smooth out the paper with the paper knife.*

6 *Spread glue over the lip and top of the moulding and fold the strip of paper up over them. Gently smooth out the paper with the paper knife.*

7 *Repeat in the same way for each surface of the moulding, including the rebate, applying glue as you go.*

8 *Repeat for the three other pieces of moulding. Leave to dry for 30 minutes.*

Assembling the moulding

1 *Using scissors, carefully cut off the excess paper from each end of the moulding.*

2 *Assemble the lengths of moulding to make the frame, following the instructions on page 29, steps 9 to 13. As the moulding is covered with paper you don't need to sand the corners.*

Final assembly

1 *To fix the clips in place, place the frame face down on the work surface, place the scale rule along one side of the frame, and make a pilot hole in the centre with the bradawl.*

2 *Repeat for the other three sides of the frame.*

Tip

To gauge the depth of the pilot holes, use the screws of the clips as a guide. Align a screw against the bradawl and, with a felt-tip pen, mark the length of the screw on it. If the hole is too deep, the screw will not hold.

3 *Insert the glass – spotlessly clean – into the frame, followed by the photo and the backing board, with the covered side visible.*

4 *Screw each clip into the pilot holes already made.*

5 *For the hanging attachment, make a hole with the bradawl in the middle of the back of the frame at the top. Screw in the eye.*

DOUBLE OR TRIPTYCH PHOTO FRAME

A double or triptych photo frame looks good placed on a table, mantelpiece or shelf. It consists of two or three identical frames fixed together by means of two small metal hinges screwed into the back of the frames. The following instructions are for either a double or triptych frame.

Tip

Hinges come in a range of sizes. Use larger ones for larger frames, but always choose a hinge narrower than the moulding. Buy brass hinges, with the necessary fixing nails or screws.

MATERIALS

2 or 3 identical frames
Backing board, covered to
match the frames
Metal scale rule
Bradawl
Small clips
2 or 4 hinges
Small nails
Hammer
2 or 3 pieces of glass

Method

1 Make up two or three frames, referring to the instructions on pages 27–9.

2 Cut backing boards for each frame to the required dimensions.

3 Position the frames side by side, face down, on the work surface.

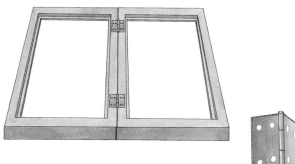

4 Join the frames together with the hinges. For each pair, fix one hinge 1 in (2.5 cm) from the top of the frames and the other 1 in (2.5 cm) from the bottom. Nail or screw in place, using the holes provided.

5 For the final assembly, see the previous section, 'A simple photo frame' on pages 114–116.

PHOTO FRAME WITH MULTIPLE WINDOWS

An attractive way of displaying various photos of children and families is to put them together in a single frame, using a mount with two or more windows. To give an impression of depth to your arrangement, make the mount from thick mountboard, which you can then cover in fabric or paper, or give a paint effect.

Frames with multiple windows
can be used for displaying collections of
dried plants or arrangements of
seeds or shells, as well as for pictures.
You can also use plain mounting
card for a simpler mount, if your
items don't need extra depth.

MATERIALS

Frame	Cutter
Glass	Metal scale rule
Mountboard	Heavy ruler
Brown gummed paper tape	6 large clips
Backing board	1 screw eye
Paper to cover the backing board	Cloth
	Small screwdriver
Acrylic paint in 2 colours	Bradawl
Paintbrush	

Method

1 *Cut the backing board and the mountboard to the chosen dimensions. Make up the frame (see pages 27–9) and paint it.*

2 *Mark the dimensions of the windows on the mountboard, allowing a wider margin between the windows and the borders of the mount. Cut them out using a cutter and heavy ruler, following the instructions in 'Framing with a mount' on pages 32–4.*

3 *Paint the mount and leave it to dry for 30 minutes. Alternatively, cover it with fabric or paper (see 'Framing with a mount: Covering a mount' on pages 36–8). Cover the visible side of the backing board with paper.*

4 *Position the photos, sticking them to the back of the mount with small pieces of brown gummed paper tape.*

5 *For the final assembly, refer to 'Simple photo frame: Final assembly' on page 116, steps 1 to 5.*

MULTIPLE PHOTO MOUNT WITH DIFFERENT-SHAPED WINDOWS

This project uses a ready-cut multiple mount with windows of various shapes: oval, round, hexagonal, rectangular and square. The instructions are for covering this type of mount with fabric.

Tip

Given the difficulty of cutting out a large number of windows in circles, ovals or with rounded corners, you can buy a ready-cut mount (generally black) and decorate it with paper or fabric.

MATERIALS

Frame	Cutter
Glass	Metal scale rule
Backing board	Heavy ruler
1 multiple-window mount	Paper knife
Fabric to cover the mount and backing board	Brown gummed paper
	1 screw eye
PVA adhesive	Bradawl
Flat paintbrush	Screwdriver

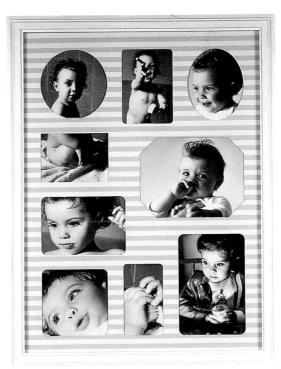

Method

1 *Cut a backing board to the dimensions of the mount.*

2 *Make the frame and decorate it as you wish.*

3 *Apply glue to one side of the mount.*

4 *Place the fabric face down on the work surface. Place the glued side of the mount on the fabric. Press down firmly with the palm of the hand. Check that the fabric is well stretched, and pull out any creases. Place it under a press for an hour.*

5 *Cut out the window openings in the fabric. For shapes with angled corners, make cuts at each corner, referring to 'Framing with a mount: Covering a mount', on pages 36–8.*

6 *For round and oval openings, cut the fabric to about ¾ in (18 mm) from the edge of the window. Using the cutter, make a series of cuts into the fabric, to form a fringe round the shape, taking the cuts almost to the edge of the window.*

7 *Apply glue to each tiny wedge of fabric, and fold it to the back of the mount using the paper knife.*

Tip

If the wedges of fabric are too wide to fold back neatly, the window won't have a smooth edge.

8 *Gently run the tip of the paper knife around the edge of the window openings to make the edges as regular as possible.*

9 *Apply glue to one side of the backing board and cover it in the same fabric as the mount, trimming the edges.*

10 *Once the coverings are complete, place the mount and backing board under a press for two hours.*

11 *Cut the photos so that they are slightly larger than the windows, and stick them in place at the back of the mount using ¾-in (18-mm) pieces of gummed brown paper.*

Tip

Before sticking the photos in place, make sure that they are properly centred in the windows.

12 *For the final assembly, see 'A simple photo frame: Final assembly' on page 116.*

MULTIPLE MOUNT WITH OLD-STYLE FRAME

This project is a quick and easy way of using an old frame to display photos. The photos are inserted side by side into supporting rows of covered mounting card. The number of rows depends on the height of the frame and personal choice. In the example shown here, the width of each row is 4 in (10 cm), while the bottom row is the width of the residual space.

This example uses a traditional frame, but has a deliberately informal and modern arrangement inside it, with the striped mount and no glass.

Tip

If you are working with an old frame, carefully take its measurements before cutting the mount strips to size.

MATERIALS

Frame	Paper knife
Backing board	PVA adhesive
Plain mounting card	Pencil
Fabric to cover the mount	Cloth
and backing board	Bradawl
Metal scale rule	6 large clips
Heavy ruler	Screwdriver
Cutter	1 screw eye

Method

1 *Cut a backing board to fit the back of the frame. Apply glue to one side of the board and cover it with fabric. Although this side will be at the back of the frame, it is covered for a perfect finish.*

2 *Mark the measurements of the strips on the mounting card and cut them out.*

3 *Cut strips of fabric ⅞ in (2 cm) longer and wider than the cut pieces of mounting card.*

Tip

If using striped or checked fabric, cut some of the strips in line with its design and others in the other direction.

4 *Place a strip of fabric face down on the work surface. Apply glue to one side of a card strip.*

5 *Stick the card to the fabric with a margin on all four sides. Smooth down the fabric with the palm of your hand and the paper knife. Turn it over and smooth down again.*

6 To fold the fabric over along the top, make two diagonal cuts across the top two corners of the fabric.

7 Apply glue to the strip of fabric to be turned over. Pull the fabric taut, fold over and stick to the back of the card. Remove any residual glue with the paper knife.

8 Place the strip, fabric side down, on the work surface. Cut away the remaining three sides along the edge of the mount, using the cutter and heavy ruler.

9 Repeat in the same way to cover the other strips. Place the strips under a press for an hour.

Sticking the strips to the backing board

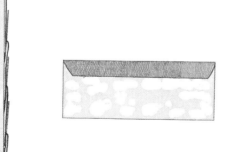

The top strip is completely glued to the uncovered side of the backing board, while the other strips are partially glued, with their top edges left free for the first ½ in (1 cm) so that the photos can be slid down behind them.

1 Apply glue to the back of the first strip and stick it to the top edge of the backing board. Press down firmly with the palm of your hand.

2 To position the second strip, make a pencil mark (using the scale rule) ½ in (1 cm) from the bottom of the first strip, at each end.

3 Apply glue to the back of the second strip, except at the top edge where the fabric has been folded back.

4 Position this second strip on the backing board, overlapping the first strip by ½ in (1 cm), using the marks made on the first strip. Smooth down with the palm of your hand.

5 Repeat steps 2 to 4 for the remaining strips.

6 Place the whole thing under a press for an hour.

7 For the final assembly, see 'A simple photo frame: Final assembly' on page 116.

Tip

Proceed in exactly the same way for any additional strips. Hang larger frames using two eyes, one on each side of the frame, with a nylon cord strung between them.

PERSPEX FRAME

The originality of a Perspex frame lies in the fact that it does not have a moulding surround. The item or items are positioned between two sheets of Perspex, held in place by bolts, in this example one at each corner.

Before buying the Perspex, measure the picture or the items you wish to frame, and allow a margin all round of at least 2 in (5 cm).

MATERIALS

2 sheets of Perspex of the required size	4 appropriately sized steel hexagonal bolts
Drill	Clean cloth

Tip

Have the Perspex cut by a specialist supplier. Choose bolts that are appropriate for the size of the frame.

Method

1 *Place the two sheets of Perspex one on top of the other, well aligned, on the work surface.*

2 *Mark the position of the holes for the bolts at each corner.*

3 *Move one of the Perspex sheets so that one side hangs beyond the edge of the work surface. Drill holes where marked.*

Tip

Check that the location marks for the holes are clear of the edge of the work surface, to prevent damaging the table with the drill. Stick double-sided adhesive tape on the back of the subject to help hold it in place between the sheets of Perspex.

4 *Repeat for the opposite side.*

5 *Remove the protective film from one of the sheets of Perspex. Clean it thoroughly with a clean cloth.*

6 *Place the cleaned sheet of Perspex on the work surface and position the subject to be framed in the centre.*

7 *Remove the protective film from the second sheet of Perspex and clean it.*

8 *Position the second sheet over the first and put the bolts in place. Gently move the frame so it overhangs the edge of the table to enable you to tighten the bolts.*

BYZANTINE-STYLE MULTIPLE FRAME

This is an interesting style of multiple photo frame. Unlike other types of frame, here the photos cannot be moved, as they are fixed in place on the backing board. A decorative moulding separates each photo. The moulding around the central photo may be wider than the rest, but they should all be in the same style. The wide moulding of the frame surrounding the pictures has some detail on it that echoes the pattern on the internal mouldings.

This multiple frame would be ideal for family photos in the form of a family tree. The photos are behind glass, the first element to go into the frame, followed by the backing board with the Byzantine-style arrangement.

To begin with, follow the instructions for this example. The central frame contains a large photo, which is surrounded by ten smaller images, eight of which are the same size and two of which are slightly larger. The moulding of the central frame is ⅞ in (2 cm) wide, that separating the smaller pictures is ¾ in (1.8 cm). The exterior frame moulding is just under 3 in (7.5 cm) wide. The inner mouldings are painted gold and the outer frame is blue.

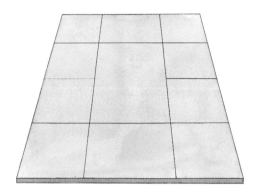

MATERIALS

Backing board	Fine glasspaper
Metal scale rule	Sponges with and without
Heavy ruler	scourer
Mitre box and saw, or	Red, blue and gold paint
frame saw	Neoprene glue
H or HB pencil	Glass
Cutter	Nails
PVA adhesive	Brown gummed paper
Paintbrush	tape
¾, ⅞ and 3-in (1.8, 2 and	Bradawl
7.5-cm) mouldings	2 screw eyes
Emery board	Cord

Measuring and cutting the backing board

Choose your photos and measure them. In this example, there are four photos down each side of the arrangement, all 3½ × 3½ in (9 × 9 cm). Down the middle are three photos, two of them 5 × 3½ in (13 × 9 cm), and a double-height photo, 5 × 7 in (13 × 18 cm), in the centre.

1 *To calculate the dimensions of the backing board, arrange the photos in position and add up their measurements. The total width here is 12 in (31 cm); the total height is 14 in (36 cm). Cut the backing board to these dimensions.*

𝒯 i p

It is important to choose the pictures carefully. With family photos, for example, you could put grandparents in the middle, surrounded by the children and grandchildren. With holiday photos, place a view of the location in the centre with activities or places visited around the outside. For photos of a child, put a baby photo in the centre, surrounded by pictures of him or her at different ages.

2 *On the backing board mark in pencil the dimensions of the photos, starting with the ones along top and bottom, then the five in the middle. Join the marks to outline the positioning of the pictures.*

3 *If your photos are not all quite the right size, cut them to the required dimensions if necessary.*

𝒯 i p

Before cutting photos, mark where to cut on the front of the photo with felt-tip pen, then cut using the cutter and heavy ruler.

4 *Glue the photos in place one by one. With PVA adhesive, fix the first one in position and press down well with the palm of the hand. Repeat for all the photos.*

5 *Place a piece of backing board over the photos, weight it down and leave under the press for an hour.*

Measuring and cutting the inner mouldings

1 *Start by making the central frame. Deduct ⅞ in (2 cm) from the dimensions of the largest photo, which will be covered by the moulding: 7 – ⅞ in (18 – 2 cm) and 5 – ⅞ in (13 – 2 cm) make 6⅛ × 4⅛ in (16 × 11 cm). These are the dimensions of the moulding around the central photo.*

2 *Using the mitre box and saw, or a frame saw, cut the ⅞-in (2-cm) moulding to these dimensions. First, cut the right-hand corner. Using the scale rule, mark off 6⅛ in (16 cm) and cut the second corner. Repeat this operation. Cut two further pieces 4⅛ in (11 cm) long.*

3 *For the mouldings between the smaller photos, deduct ½ in (1 cm) from 3½ in (9 cm) to make 3 in (7.5 cm).*

4 *Take a ¾-in (1.8-cm) wide piece of moulding. Position the saw to cut the ends at a right angle. Mark off 3 in (7.5 cm) in pencil on the moulding and cut it to this length.*

5 *Repeat for the other ten inner mouldings.*

Painting the mouldings and fixing them in place

1 *Take each piece of moulding and sand the cut ends with the emery board to remove any splinters. Remove all traces of sawdust with a damp sponge.*

2 *Apply two coats of red paint to each piece. Allow to dry, then apply a final coat of gold paint. To give an antique effect, lightly rub down this last coat with fine wire wool or a scourer.*

Tip

Apply two coats of paint to the cut ends of each piece so that no natural wood shows when the pieces are fixed to the backing board.

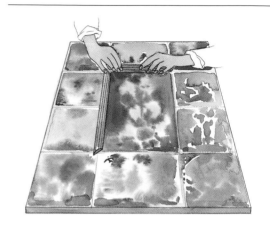

3 *Start to glue the mouldings in place around the central picture. Apply a thin line of neoprene glue centrally along the back of the first piece of moulding. Glue it in place between two of the photos. Press down well.*

4 *Repeat to fix all the mouldings in place.*

Measuring, cutting and assembling the outer frame

1 *The size of the frame is calculated on the basis of the backing board. Cut and assemble as explained in 'Simple picture framing: Measuring, cutting and assembling the moulding' on pages 27–9.*

2 *Having cut and assembled the frame, apply two coats of blue paint. Allow to dry for an hour.*

Final assembly

1 *Cut out a piece of glass ½ in (2 mm thick) to the same dimensions as the backing board: 12 × 14 in (31 × 36 cm). Clean it thoroughly.*

2 *Place the outer frame face down on the work surface. Position the glass inside it, followed by the backing board with the photos and mouldings.*

3 *Fix everything together by hammering nails (two at each corner) into the rebate of the moulding, across the backing board. Press the nails into position with the index finger and hammer them in. Add further nails spaced along the four sides, also running across the backing board.*

4 *Cut four strips of brown gummed paper tape to the length of each side of the frame. Stick each strip along the back of the frame, to seal the gap between frame and backing board. Smooth it down with the thumbs, from the centre of each strip.*

5 *Make a shallow hole with the bradawl three-quarters of the way up the back of each side of the frame, in the centre of the wood. Screw an eye firmly into these two holes.*

6 *Hang the picture on the wall by a cord tied between the two eyes.*

A FREE-STANDING FRAME

This project is for a frame that will stand up on a surface. It has a removeable back so that you can easily change the photo. This type of frame is available from framing suppliers, but only in standard sizes. The stand is attached to the backing board, and its size varies according to the size of the frame.

It is assembled only after all the elements of the frame have been made. For a neater finish, a piece of card the same size as the backing board is covered in matching paper and glued to the wrong side of the backing board. The backing board in this example measures 6½ × 9 in (17 × 24 cm).

MATERIALS

Backing board	Glue
Mounting card	Extra-strong ribbon ½ in
Bookbinding paper	(1 cm) wide
Pencil	Brown gummed paper tape
Paper knife	Strong brown adhesive tape
Tweezers	Cutter

Method

1 Cut out a backing board and a piece of mounting card to the same dimensions. Cover one side of each in your chosen paper. Set aside.

2 At the point where the hanging attachment is usually positioned (1½ in (4 cm) down from the top edge of the backing board), make a horizontal slit about 2 in (5 cm) wide. Note the height from the slit to the bottom of the board on a piece of paper, in this case 5 in (13 cm). Put the backing board to one side.

Tip

The width of the horizontal slit and the distance from it to the bottom of the backing board will vary depending on the size of the backing board. The larger this is, the wider the slit should be and the further from the bottom of the backing board.

3 To prepare the stand, mark the following dimensions on a piece of backing board:
– the top edge of the stand should be 2 in (5 cm) wide, the width of the slit cut into the backing board;
– the height of the stand is 5 in (13 cm), the distance from the slit to the bottom of the backing board;
– the bottom edge is 4 in (10 cm), for stability. Join these points with a pencil and ruler, and cut out the resulting trapezium.

4 To cover this trapezium, place it on the back of a piece of the paper used to cover the backing board, and draw round its outline in pencil.

5 Add a ½-in (1-cm) margin around all four sides and draw in with the pencil. Cut out the paper trapezium.

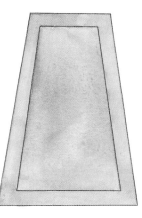

6 Glue one side of the board trapezium and place it in the outline drawn on the back of the paper. Smooth down the paper with the paper knife.

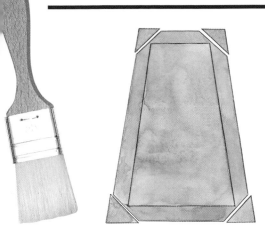

7 *Fold over the edges and glue them down over the back of the trapezium. Smooth down with the paper knife and leave to dry for 30 minutes.*

Tip

For a neat finish, cut off the corners of the paper before folding the margins down over the trapezium.

8 *Make a horizontal cut ½ in (1 cm) wide towards the base of the trapezium, ensuring that it is central.*

9 *Cut a 4-in (10 cm) length of extra-strong ribbon.*

10 *Using tweezers, thread one end of the ribbon through this slit in the stand, passing it through to the back by about ½ in (1 cm).*

11 *Glue this end of the ribbon to the board, and cover it with a piece of gummed paper tape.*

12 *Draw round the trapezium on to another piece of board. Add an additional tab 2 × 2 in (5 × 5 cm) to the top edge, which will be passed through the slit in the backing board and glued to the back, to hold the stand in place.*

13 *Cover this second trapezium (except the square tab) in the same way as the first.*

14 *Apply glue to the back of both trapeziums and stick them together to form the stand. Place under a press for 30 minutes.*

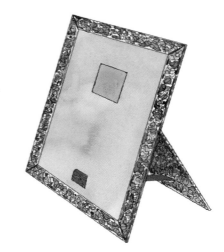

Fixing the stand to the backing board

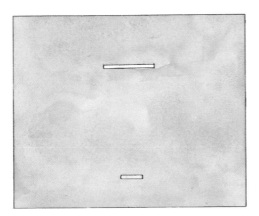

1 *Place the backing board, covered side up, on the work surface. Make a central horizontal mark 2 in (5 cm) from the bottom, ½ in (1 cm) wide (the width of the ribbon). Make a slit with the cutter.*

2 *Using the tweezers, insert the free end of the ribbon through the slit, taking care not to twist it.*

3 *Glue ½ in (1 cm) of the ribbon to the back of the backing board, and secure with a piece of gummed paper tape.*

4 *Slip the square tab of the stand through the upper slit in the backing board, and stick in place with strong brown adhesive tape.*

5 *Take the paper-covered card and stick it to the unfinished side of the backing board. Put the finished frame under a press.*

Tip

When pressing the finished backing board, place offcuts of board on each side of the stand to compensate for its thickness.

DECORATIVE IDEAS

A TRAY

An original way of using a framed picture is to make it into a tray. Use a flat moulding at least 1½ in (4 cm) wide, but not so wide as to be unwieldy. Start by making up a simple picture frame, following the instructions in 'Simple picture framing' on pages 24–31, but without fixing the hanging attachment.

MATERIALS

Finished frame	1¾-in (4.5-cm) brown
2 pieces of backing board	gummed paper tape
Metal scale rule	Clean cloth
Heavy ruler	2 handles with screws
Cutter	Drill
½-in (12-mm) nails	Hammer
Perspex	Decorative paper or fabric

To make the tray sturdier, use two layers of backing board, and top with Perspex, which is lighter and tougher than glass. Make the Perspex, picture and backing into a sealed package. Mark the position of the handles on the frame before you insert the picture package and, for extra stability, fix it into the frame with nails every 1½ in (4 cm).

The back of the tray is covered in paper or fabric, over the whole backing board and three-quarters of the back of the frame.

You can use all kinds of images for the picture element of the tray, such as architects' drawings, stencils decorating a painted piece of board, or a mosaic of photos.

Method

1 Cut two identical backing boards to the interior dimensions of the frame.

2 Position the handles on the frame and mark where the screws will go. Make pilot holes with the drill.

3 Make up the picture element of the tray, using one of the backing boards as a support.

4 Make up the picture package, including both backing boards, and insert it into the frame. Nail it firmly in place.

5 Apply glue to the backing board and to three-quarters of the back of the frame.

6 Glue in place your chosen backing paper or fabric.

7 Place the tray on the work surface and position the handles.

8 Screw the handles in place.

A FRAMED PANEL

A framed panel can be used as a notice board or for hanging earrings or brooches using pins or drawing pins.

MATERIALS

Finished frame	Metal scale rule
2 pieces of backing board	Heavy ruler
Hanging attachment	½-in (12-mm) nails
Felt	1¾-in (4.5-cm) brown
Fabric	gummed paper tape
PVA adhesive	Paper knife
Cutter	

Method

1 *Cut out two identical backing boards to fit the rebate of the frame.*

2 *Fix the hanging attachment to one of the backing boards.*

3 *Cut a piece of felt 1 in (2.5 cm) wider than the backing board. Apply adhesive to one side of the backing board without the hanging attachment. Glue the felt in place and leave to dry for four hours.*

4 *Cut out a piece of fabric 1½ in (4 cm) larger all round than the backing board, and place it face down on the work surface.*

5 *Centre the felt-covered backing board face down on the fabric. Cut away the corners of the fabric with the cutter, to just beyond each corner of the backing board.*

6 *Spread glue along the edges of the fabric. Fold down each edge over the back of the board, pulling the fabric taut and smoothing it down with the paper knife. (You need to glue the fabric edges only, because if you glue it directly to the felt it will stain.)*

7 *Position this covered backing board in the frame.*

8 *Nail the second backing board in place in the frame, and seal with strips of brown gummed paper tape, following the instructions on page 31.*

A MINIATURE DISPLAY CASE

Miniature display cases are very fashionable. Since making them involves painstaking work, and you can also make the objects to go in them, they make imaginative and inexpensive gifts with a personal touch, which will be much appreciated. Some ideas for themes include an artist's workshop, a classroom, a library, a bakery and a sewing room, as here; give free rein to your imagination.

Tip

This is an excellent way of using up scraps of fabric, card, wallpaper and other leftover materials.

The box

MATERIALS

Backing board · Cutter
Brown gummed paper tape · Paper knife
Fine glasspaper · Sponge
Metal hanging ring · PVA adhesive
Wallpaper

1 *To make an average-sized display case, cut backing board to the following dimensions:*
back: 10 × 8 in (25 × 21 cm);
long sides: 10 × 2⅔ in (25 × 6.5 cm) (two pieces);
short sides: 8 × 2½ in (21 × 6 cm) (two pieces).

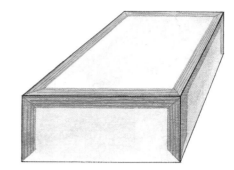

2 *Fix the hanging attachment to the back piece of board. Refer to 'Simple picture framing: Fixing the hanging attachment' on page 26.*

ASSEMBLING THE BOX

1 *Check that the pieces fit snugly by putting them together with your hands.*

3 *Start with the long sides. Stick half of each long strip to what will become the outer edges of the box, the other half to the base, edge to edge. Smooth down well with the paper knife. Repeat the procedure for the short sides and then for the four corners, with the base of the box uppermost.*

2 *Cut four 10-in (25-cm) strips of brown gummed paper tape, four 8-in (21-cm) strips and eight 2⅔-in (6.5-cm) strips. Fold these strips in half lengthways, using the paper knife. Cut a diagonal from each end of the strips as shown, so that they don't overlap when stuck in place.*

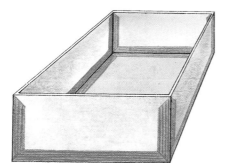

4 *Stick the remaining strips of tape in place inside the box.*

𝒯 i p

Smooth out any creases in the tape, which might show through the decorative covering.

LINING AND COVERING THE BOX

The box is lined and covered with wallpaper, bookbinding paper or fabric.

1 *Cut two strips of wallpaper 28 in (72 cm) long by 2⅔ in (6.5 cm) wide for three sides and two strips 8 × 2⅔ in (21 × 6.5 cm) for the fourth side. Apply glue to one longer strip. Fit it to two long and one short interior sides, starting with a long side. Take a short strip, and stick it to the remaining interior side. Smooth down with the paper knife and a cloth. Use the remaining strips of paper to cover the outer sides of the box in the same way.*

2 *Next, cut out a rectangle of wallpaper to fit the base of the box. Spread it with glue and stick it to the base, working from top to bottom. Smooth down well with the paper knife.*

Sewing room display

Most of the objects in this display are home-made, but some are from specialist retailers.

MAKING THE DISPLAY ITEMS

Shelves

1 *From backing board cut one shelf 10 × 1½ in (25 × 4 cm), and another 3½ × 1½ in (9 × 4 cm).*

2 *Cover them in the same wallpaper as the box, including the edges.*

Table

1 *From backing board cut out a rectangle 2¾ × 1⅛ in (7 × 3 cm) and another 2¾ × 1⅖ in (7 × 3.5 cm). Next, cut a 2¾-in (7-cm) length of gummed paper tape and assemble the pieces to make a right angle. Stick tape along the inside of the angle.*

2 *Cover the table with the same or contrasting wallpaper.*

Fabric rolls

1 *Cut 25 strips measuring 1 × 1½ in (2.5 × 4 cm) out of various fabrics, wallpapers and thick white paper.*

𝒯 i p

Draw your own designs on the paper with coloured felt-tip pens.

2 *Cut 25 strips of backing board measuring 1⅛ × ¼ in (3 × 0.5 cm) for rolling up the pieces of fabric and paper. Apply glue to one side of the board, position it on the fabric and roll it up. Glue down the end of the roll.*

Balls of wool

Take lengths of thick thread and roll them up into small balls. Make about eight balls of different colours.

Reels of sewing thread

Cut matchsticks into ½-in (1-cm) pieces. Wind round threads of different colours.

Button box

Cut two rectangles of thick white paper measuring 1 × ⅞ in (2.5 cm × 2 cm). Place the rectangles on top of each other and glue together. Fold up the four sides, using the paper knife, to form a box. Make another box with coloured paper.

Arranging the items in the box

Shelves

Make four small battens 1⅛ in (3 cm) long, from a piece of balsa moulding. For the long shelf, glue a batten to each side wall of the box, 2 in (5 cm) from the top.
For the smaller shelf, glue one batten on the left-hand wall 3½ in (9 cm) from the top and the second at the same height on the back wall 2½ in (6 cm) in from the side. Glue the shelves to the battens.

Table

From the balsa make a batten 2⅗ in (6.5 cm) long and a second 1 in (2.5 cm) long. Glue the longer batten to the inside angle of the table and the shorter one to the right-hand wall of the box at the height of the table. Glue the table to it.

Reels of sewing thread and buttons

Glue them in place in the two little paper boxes, and glue the boxes to the smaller shelf, along with a roll of fabric.

Balls of wool

Glue them into a little shallow dish, and glue this to the base of the box. Next to this dish place a ball of wool with some knitting needles (made from shortened pins).

Rolls of fabric

1 *Place seven rows of two or three rolls on the top shelf, arranged diagonally and glued to one another.*

2 *Glue four rolls of fabric against the left-hand wall at the base of the box. If using other, bought, objects, fix them in place with a spot of glue.*

Final assembly

1 *For the frame, choose a moulding and refer to 'Simple picture framing' on pages 27–9 to make it up.*

2 *Have the glass cut to the precise dimensions of the frame.*

Tip

It's important to take the precise measurements of the box before making the frame and having the glass cut.

3 *Carefully clean the glass before placing it in the frame.*

4 *Place the box in the frame and check that none of the objects has come loose.*

5 *To attach the box to the frame, cut strips of brown gummed paper tape, folded lengthways, and stick them over the gaps between box and frame.*

A BAROQUE-STYLE DISPLAY

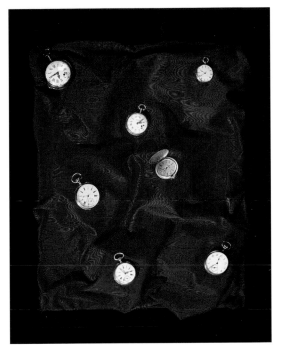

Baroque-style framing is an unusual way of displaying several small framed pictures or other objects within a large frame, or of giving added impact to collectors' items.

Your main frame can either be one you found in a junk shop or attic, or one you make yourself using a wide, antique-style moulding. The small framed pictures or other items can be in any style, perhaps a little worn-looking to emphasise the baroque feel of the ensemble. The backing board is covered in fairly thick fabric with a silky or iridescent finish (such as moiré or taffeta) in red, green or deep yellow. This is draped to give a relief effect, accentuated by crumpled pieces of kraft paper glued to the backing board underneath. A ¼-in (6-mm) thick piece of plywood is fitted to the back of the frame, between two sheets of backing board, to take the small nails used for fixing the items in place within the large frame.

MATERIALS

Mitre box and saw or frame saw	Brown paper
3¼ to 4¾-in (8 to 12-cm) wide moulding	Brown gummed paper tape
	Sponge
	¼-in (6-mm) plywood
2 pieces of backing board	Small nails
Moiré fabric	Long nails
PVA adhesive	Bradawl
Brush	2 screw eyes
Black felt-tip pen	Cord.

Method

Decide on the size of the large frame and the objects you wish to display. In this example, the backing board is ¹⁄₁₀ in (3 mm) thick and measures 32 × 25 in (80 × 65 cm). The little frames vary in size and shape. Some are second-hand, others home-made. They should not be too heavy.

Choose a moulding at least 3 in (7.5 cm) wide for the main frame. For an original effect, leave some of the smaller frames empty, and hang medals or trinkets inside them.

1 *Mark the dimensions of the backing board, and cut it to size with the cutter and heavy ruler. Cut a second backing board to the same size.*

2 *Have a piece of plywood cut to the same size as the backing boards.*

Plywood is sold by picture framing suppliers and at DIY or hardware stores.

3 *Cut and assemble the main frame. If using a frame saw, refer to 'Multiple frames: Cutting the mouldings' on pages 85–6, steps 2 to 4 and 7. If using a mitre box, refer to 'Simple picture framing: Measuring, cutting and assembling the moulding' on pages 27–9, steps 1 to 14.*

4 *Cut a piece of your chosen fabric to 40 × 34 in (100 × 85 cm), and set aside.*

5 *Cut about 20 rectangles of brown paper of different sizes. Crumple them up into different shapes and volumes.*

Use quite thick, stiff kraft paper; this will give greater relief and support to the fabric.

6 *With a moistened brush, spread PVA adhesive over one side of a backing board.*

To moisten the brush, dip it in water and squeeze out before using.

7 *Quickly spread the crumpled pieces of brown paper over the backing board.*

8 *Place the fabric face down on the work surface, protected by a piece of board. Spread PVA adhesive over the back of the fabric with the brush.*

9 *Add more glue to any parts of the backing board where the original glue has dried. Place the fabric, glued side down, on the backing board prepared with the balls of brown paper. Where there is no brown paper, press it down with the palm of your hand. Gently fluff out the fabric where it lies over the balls of brown paper so that it assumes their shape. Leave to dry for half an hour.*

You can rearrange the creases and folds in the fabric several times to achieve the desired effect.

10 *Place the main frame face down on the work surface and insert the fabric-covered backing board into it.*

11 *Nail the corners of the frame, passing the nails through the backing board into the inner face of the rebate. Push the nails through the board with your index finger, then drive them into the wood with the hammer. Hammer in nails every 2 in (5 cm) all round the frame, through the backing board.*

12 *Next, place the plywood in position. Hammer nails well into the rebate at the corners, positioning them flat against the plywood. Hammer in more nails around the frame.*

13 *Turn the whole thing face up on the work surface and arrange the little frames at random on the fabric.*

14 *With a felt-tip pen, lightly mark the location of the nails for attaching the objects.*

Tip

To mark the location of the nails, tilt each little frame up slightly, just enough to insert the pen and make a mark. Remove the frame once the mark is made.

15 *Take the shorter nails. Hammer each one into place (through the fabric, backing board and plywood) but not completely, so that the object can be hung on it.*

16 *Place the frame face down on the work surface and cut off the projecting points at the back with pliers.*

17 *Place the second backing board in the frame, over the plywood. Nail it in place in the same way as the first.*

18 *Cut a strip of brown gummed paper tape to the length of the frame. Position one end, glue side down, on a damp sponge and draw it across with one hand, keeping it pressed down with your other hand.*

19 *Stick the moistened tape over the gap between the backing board and the frame, placing it first on the back of the moulding and smoothing it down with the thumbs, starting in the middle. Repeat for the other three sides.*

20 *Make a mark with a bradawl three-quarters of the way up one side of the back of the frame. Deepen to form a pilot hole, then screw in an eye until firmly in place. Fix the second eye in place on the other side.*

21 *Hang the frame on the wall by a cord tied between the two eyes.*

SOME UNUSUAL IDEAS

Picture border

Materials
- Mountboard ● Small pictures
- HB or H pencil ● Rotring pen
- Brown Rotring ink ● Eraser

You can use all kinds of small pictures cut from magazines to make a border decoration for a mount, including faces, photos of animals or objects, or old advertisements.

Proceed in the same way as for the flowery borders described on pages 108–109. Follow the step-by-step instructions, replacing the flowers with your chosen photos.

You can vary the width of the decorated band and the ink lines to suit your taste and the size of the mount.

Fabric-wrapped frame

Materials
- Round frame with octagonal inner opening (found in a second-hand shop) ● Fabric ● Clear wax ● Upholstery tacks
- Yellow and orange pigment ● Cotton wool

1. Cut enough strips of fabric to wrap around the frame. Fix the ends of each strip to the back of the frame with tacks. Take care to ensure that the end of the last strip finishes at the back of the frame.

2. Make a suitable mount (see pages 32–5). Tip a little of each pigment on to an offcut of card. Using a cotton wool ball, spread a coat of yellow pigment over the mount, followed by a coat of orange. Remove the surplus with a clean piece of cotton wool. Apply a coat of wax with a cloth.

3. Assemble without glass, checking that the picture is properly centred. Nail the edge of the backing board to the frame.

Pinewood frame

Materials
● Flat, natural wood moulding 2¾ in (7 cm) wide ● Green paint ● Matt varnish ● Patina wood finish (product for giving an ageing effect to wood) ● Wood shavings (from pot pourri) ● Superglue

1. Use the moulding to make a simple frame (see pages 24–9). Paint the frame and leave it to dry.

2. Mix together one part patina with two parts varnish in a suitable receptacle. Apply this mixture to the frame with a flat brush and leave to dry before undertaking the final assembly. Glue the wood shavings around the frame using superglue.

Forest frame

Materials
● 12 twiggy sticks of different shapes and sizes
● Earth-coloured pigment ● Fine green wire
● Pine cones, pieces of bark, husks, etc.
● PVA adhesive ● Cotton wool

1. Make a mount for your chosen picture and attach (see pages 32–5). Decide how wide you want the decorated border to be, and add these measurements to the area of the mounted picture to obtain the dimensions of the backing board.

2. Tip a little pigment on to a piece of card. Using a cotton wool ball, colour the mount. Tap the back of the mount to remove surplus pigment.

3. Use the wire to assemble the pieces of wood in groups of three. Wrap the wire round each end a few times and leave an extra 1½-in (4-cm) length of wire spare.

4. Place the twig bundles on the mount and mark the position of the wire in the four corners. Make a little hole through the mount and backing board. To fix the twig bundles in place, pass the ends of the wire through the holes and twist them together in pairs at the back. Complete the decoration of the backing board frame by gluing on pine cones, pieces of bark, fruits and other decorative pieces around the twigs.

Wheat ear border

Materials

● Moulded frame in natural wood 1 in (2.5 cm) wide ● Glass ● Balsa moulding ● Pale cream Ingres paper ● Gold paint ● Green ink ● 8 ears of wheat ● Fine glasspaper

1. Use the Ingres paper to make a mount (see pages 32–4). Make up a simple frame (see pages 24–9). Sand it down with fine glasspaper, then apply two coats of gold paint, allowing each coat an hour to dry. Apply a coat of green ink, and leave to dry.

2. Glue the ears of wheat around the mount. Place the frame face down on the work surface, and cut two pieces of balsa moulding for each side of the frame (assemble the pairs on top of one another).

3. Place the glass in the frame. Apply glue to two sides of the balsa mouldings and position them in the frame against the rebate and the glass. Assemble the frame.

A seaside theme

Materials

● Moulded frame in natural wood, 1½ in (4 cm) wide ● Balsa moulding ● Royal blue and white paint ● Natural split-wood blind ● PVA adhesive ● Differently coloured shells

1. Measure the two pictures and decide on the widths of the margins and the space between them. Add these dimensions together to obtain the size of the backing board and blind.

2. Make up a simple frame (see pages 24–9). Sand it down until smooth and remove sawdust with a damp sponge. Apply two coats of royal blue paint, leaving an hour between coats. Paint the blind white. Once it is dry, stick the two pictures and shells to it.

3. Place the frame face down on the work surface, and cut two pieces of balsa moulding for each side of the frame (assemble the pairs on top of one another). Apply glue to two sides of the balsa mouldings and position them in the frame against the rebate and the glass. Position the elements in the frame and assemble.

Out of Africa

Materials
● Strips of brown upholstery fabric
● Glass ● PVA adhesive

1. Cut backing board to the dimensions of the picture. Assemble the glass, picture and backing board (see pages 30–31).

2. Cut four strips of upholstery fabric, one for each side of the picture package, and wide enough to wrap round to the back.

3. Apply adhesive to one strip. Place one long edge on the glass and press down with the thumbs, from the middle to the ends. Repeat several times. Press the fabric over the edge and round to the backing board. Glue the opposite band in the same way, and press overnight. Finish the remaining sides the next day.

Lions and cats

Materials

● Imitation mahogany moulding 1 in (2.5 cm) wide ● Imitation leopardskin fabric ● Orange and sienna pigments ● Clear wax ● Cat's head stickers

1. Make two slip mounts (see pages 39–40), one 1½ in (4 cm) narrower than the other. Cover the wider one with fabric (see pages 36–8).

2. Using a cotton wool ball, apply a coat of orange then a coat of sienna pigment to the second mount. Remove the residue with clean cotton wool, and apply a coat of wax.

3. Make up a simple frame (see pages 24–9). Assemble all the elements (see page 38, steps 1 and 2). Stick the cat stickers at regular intervals around the frame.

Big cat square (page 146, bottom)

Materials

● Matching patterned mouldings 1 in (2.5 cm) wide, half salmon-pink and half black ● Pale cream Ingres paper ● 4 big cat stickers

1. Measure your picture and decide on the width of the margins of the mount. Make a square mount from the Ingres paper, cutting a square window on the diagonal as shown, and position the picture (see pages 32–5). Cut the backing board and glass to size. Make up a simple frame (see pages 30–31).

2. Stick the big cat stickers to the mount, and assemble the frame.

Holiday memento

Materials

● Thick, flat wooden moulding ⅞ in (2 cm) wide ● Modelling plaster ● Ultramarine pigment ● Shells and pieces of coral ● 4 clips

1. Make up a simple frame (see pages 24–9). Fix a clip to each side of the frame to hold the backing board in place. To do this, make a pilot hole with a bradawl in the centre of the moulding and screw in the clip. For the hanging attachment, make a hole in the centre of the top moulding and screw in an eye.

2. In a suitable receptacle mix up some plaster and pigment, adding enough water to make a thick but malleable paste. Using your hands, cover the frame with the plaster. Place a piece of coral at each corner and shells around the sides. Leave to dry for several hours.

3. Insert the glass, photo and backing board in the frame. Hold them in place with the clips.

On the beach

Materials

● Flat wooden moulding ⅞ in (2 cm) wide ● Bevelling board ● Modelling plaster ● Blue pigment ● Royal blue paint ● Yellow papyrus

1. Make up a simple frame and a bevelled mount (see pages 42–6). Apply two coats of royal blue paint to the bevelled edge, and then cover the mount with the papyrus.

2. Mix two parts plaster to one part blue pigment, adding enough water to make a thick but malleable paste. With your hands, coat the frame with this plaster, and leave to dry. Assemble the picture.

Frame with sweets

Materials

● Ornate wooden moulding 2¾ in (7 cm) wide ● White paint ● Superglue ● Translucent wrapped sweets

1. Make up a framed picture in the usual way (see pages 24–31), but before the final assembly, apply two coats of white paint to the mouldings. Allow to dry for an hour after each coat.

2. Arrange the sweets on the frame and glue in place.

Seashells

Materials

● 2 pieces of blue fluted moulding 1½ in (4 cm) wide ● 2 pieces of white decorative moulding 2 in (5 cm) wide ● Neoprene glue and superglue ● Balsa moulding ● 3 pearlescent shells

1. Cut the four pieces of moulding to the same length and assemble them (see 'Simple picture framing' on pages 27–9). Turn the frame upside down and insert the glass.

2. Cut four pieces of balsa moulding to the interior dimensions of the frame. Apply neoprene glue to these and position them in the frame to hold the glass in place. Leave to dry for several hours. Turn the frame and glass over, and glue the shells diagonally across the glass with the superglue.

In the desert

Materials
- Flat moulding 2¾ in (7 cm) wide
- Flat pieces of stone, marble and granite
- Gravel ● Matt varnish ● Superglue

1. Make up a simple frame (see pages 24–9). Sand down the frame and remove any dust with a damp sponge. Apply a coat of varnish and allow to dry. Assemble all the picture elements into the frame (see pages 30–31).

2. Break the pieces of stone to create a mosaic. Apply a layer of glue to the moulding and arrange the mosaic pieces on it. Sprinkle gravel in the empty spaces.

Dog frame

Materials
- Photos ● Slightly rounded wooden moulding 1⅜ in (3.5 cm) wide
- Dog's head stickers ● Matt varnish
- PVA adhesive ● Purple paint

1. Arrange the photos to form a rectangle. Measure them and cut two pieces of backing board to these dimensions. Glue the photos to one of these and put under a press for two hours.

2. Make up a simple frame (see pages 24–9). Sand down the frame and remove any dust with a damp sponge. Apply two coats of paint, allowing each coat an hour to dry. Assemble the picture elements into the frame (see pages 30–31).

3. Stick the dog pictures in place, and give the whole frame a coat of varnish.

Alphabet frame

Materials
- Flat moulding in natural wood ⅞ in (2 cm) wide ● Letter transfers in different styles ● Gesso ● Purple pigment

1. Make up a simple frame (see pages 24–9). Sand down the frame and apply two coats of gesso, leaving an hour between coats.

2. Tip some pigment on to a piece of card, then dab it over the frame with cotton wool. Remove any residue by tapping the back of the frame.

3. Transfer the letters on to the frame and, where appropriate, the picture surround. Assemble.

Variations on a Bear Theme

Multicoloured mount

Materials
● Rounded moulding in natural wood 1⅛ in (3 cm) wide ● 3 sheets of papyrus (green, blue and yellow) ● Yellow ink ● PVA adhesive

1. Make up a simple frame and mount (see pages 24–35). Sand down the frame, remove any dust with a damp sponge, and stain with one coat of undiluted yellow ink.

2. Cover the mount with torn pieces of papyrus. Place under a press for two hours before assembling the frame.

Cardboard mount

Materials
● Flat moulding in natural wood 1⅛ in (3 cm) wide ● Thick aluminium foil ● Corrugated cardboard ● PVA adhesive

1. Make up a simple frame and mount (see pages 24–35). Sand down the frame and remove any dust with a damp sponge.

2. Cut four strips of corrugated card, which will be used to cover the the mount. Roughly cut one edge of each strip (where it will border the window). Apply glue to the mount, and gently stick down the card (without pressing). Assemble all the picture elements into the frame.

3. Screw the foil into balls and stick them to the frame.

Butterflies

Materials
● Frame made from antique-style gilded moulding 2 in (5 cm) wide, or second-hand frame ● Backing board ● Green papyrus ● Butterfly pictures ● PVA adhesive ● Fine chicken wire

1. Cut out two pieces of backing board to fit the rebate of the frame. Cover one with the papyrus. Cut out the butterflies and stick them to the papyrus. Place under a press for an hour.

2. Cut the wire to the dimensions of the backing board. Assemble, placing the elements in the frame in the following order: the wire, the backing board with the butterflies and the second backing board.

Coloured pasta frame (page 152, bottom)

Materials
- Sloping wooden moulding 2 in (5 cm) wide ● Royal blue, red, yellow and orange paints ● Penne pasta ● Wooden toothpicks ● 1 grapefruit ● Superglue

1. Make up a simple frame (see pages 24–9). Apply two coats of royal blue paint, leaving each coat to dry for an hour.

2. Stick the toothpicks into the grapefruit. Thread the pieces of pasta on to the toothpicks and give them two coats of yellow, red or orange paint. Glue them to the frame.

Painters' frame

Materials
- Natural wood moulding 1⅛ in (3 cm) wide ● Tiled-effect moulding in natural wood 1⅛ in (3 cm) wide ● Blue, red and white paints ● ⅞-in (2-cm) nails

1. Make two simple frames the same size, one from each moulding (see pages 24–9). Sand them down and remove any dust with a damp sponge.

2. Apply two coats of blue paint to the tile-effect moulding and one of white paint to the other. An hour later, apply a thin coat of red paint to the white, to make pink. When the paint is dry, assemble glass, picture and backing board, and insert into the frame.

3. Nail the frames together as shown, sinking the nail heads into the wood. Apply another coat of blue paint to the top frame to hide the nails.

Baby's first shirt (page 154, top)

Materials
- White lacquered moulding ⅞ in (2 cm) wide
- Glass ● Baby's shirt

Measure the height and width of the garment and decide how wide to have the margins around it. Make up a double-glazed frame (see pages 68–70) to the chosen size.

Baby's bootees (page 154, bottom)

Materials
- Flat moulding in natural wood ⅞ in (2 cm) wide
- Matt white paint ● White Ingres paper ● Pair of bootees

Make up a simple frame (see pages 24–9), and paint it white. Cut the backing board and white paper to the same dimensions. Centre the bootees on the white paper and glue them in position. Assemble in the frame.

Child's frame

Materials
- 2 pieces of ornate frame moulding 1⅜ in (3.5 cm) wide
- 2 pieces of beaded moulding 1⅛ in (3 cm) wide
- Balsa moulding ● Neoprene glue ● Blue pigment
- Gloss varnish

1. Cut two pieces of each moulding, all to the same length, and assemble them. Take the internal dimensions of the frame and add ½ in (1 cm) to each side to obtain the dimensions of the backing board. Make the mount (see pages 32–4).

2. Colour the mount with a coat of pigment, then varnish it. Allow to dry, then place under a press for an hour.

3. Place the frame face down on the work surface. Cut four pieces of balsa moulding to fit the rebate of the frame. Insert the glass in the frame, then glue the balsa mouldings against the glass and the rebate. Leave to dry for an hour.

4. Fix the picture to the mount and place it, with the backing board, over the back of the frame. Attach with nails through the backing board and the back of the frame. Seal with brown gummed paper tape.

Baby's bib

Materials
- Contoured white moulding 1 in (2.5 cm) wide ● Glass ● Baby's bib

1. Measure the height and width of the bib. Add a 2-in (5-cm) margin at the bottom and 1½ in (3 cm) at the sides and top. Make up a double-glazed frame (see pages 68–70) based on these measurements.

Baby dolls (page 156, top)

Materials
- White lacquered frame moulding 1⅛ in (3 cm) wide ● Glass
- Balsa moulding ● 5 pink plastic baby dolls ● PVA adhesive
- Neoprene glue ● Rectangular paper doily ● White Ingres paper

1. Glue the paper doily to the Ingres paper, cut to the width of the margins you require. Cut the backing board to the same size.

2. Make up a simple frame (see pages 24–9). Place it face down on the work surface and insert the glass. Cut two pieces of balsa moulding to fit each side of the interior of the frame (assemble pairs on top of one another). Apply neoprene glue to two sides of each balsa pair and glue them to each side of the frame. Leave to dry for several hours.

3. Using the PVA adhesive, glue the dolls to the paper doily. Insert the paper with the dolls, then the backing board, into the frame, and fix into place (see page 31).

Aristocats (page 156, bottom)

Materials
- Gilded moulded frame 2 in (5 cm) wide ● Bevelling board
- Mounting card ● PVA adhesive ● Decorative paper
- Royal blue paint

1. Measure the picture and make up an reverse bevelled mount (see page 48, steps 3 to 6).

2. Apply two coats of paint to the bevelled edges, going over on to the flat surface. Calculate the distance you want between the reverse bevel and the octagonal window, and between the octagonal window and the edge of the frame. Add these measurements, and cut to size a backing board, a piece of bevelling board and a piece of mounting card for the background.

3. Make the outer mount with octagonal bevelled window (see pages 55–7). Paint the bevelled edges. Spread glue over the mounting card for the background and cover with decorative paper. Make up a simple frame (see pages 27–9).

4. Stick the picture to the reverse bevelled mount, and glue it in position on the mounting card. Glue decorative paper to the mount with octagonal window, and glue this in position on to the mounting card. Place the frame face down on the work surface, and assemble all the elements.

INDEX

Acknowledgements

The author would like to thank the following for their valuable help:

Anne la Fay, Dominique Raynal and Stéphanie Vinet;
Sylvie Vernichon, photographer, for her originality and kindness;
Maëlle de Mantille, who lent me some of her creations;
Laurence Ribes, Béatrice Fages and Isabelle Delarue, who helped in making the frames.

The magazine *Éclat de Verre* for the loan of accessories.
Guinée Derriaz, marble, granite and stone, Chilly-Mazarin.
Pièces Uniques, 10 Rue Bouchut, 75015 Paris, for the pocket watches.
Établissements Perucca Frère, 110 Rue Castagnary, 75015 Paris, for the glass and mirrors.

Photo credits

Cover photos: Sylvie Vernichon.
Laurent Bianquis: p. 6, p. 9, p. 12, p. 27, p. 33 (small photo), p. 36, p. 38, p. 39, p. 41, p. 43, p. 47, p. 63, p. 65 (small photo), p. 67 (bottom), p. 70, p. 98, p. 115, p. 116, p. 117, p. 119 (top), p. 121, p. 123 (bottom), p. 132, p. 133, p. 134, p. 135, p. 136.
Sylvie Vernichon: p. 8, p. 25, p. 33 (large photo), p. 50, p. 51, p. 52, p. 53, p. 54, p. 55 (picture uses 'Pogs' by Spirou de Panini, © Dupuis, TF1, Ciné-Groupe, 1995), p. 59, p. 61, p. 65 (large photo), p. 67 (top), p. 69, p. 71, p. 72, p. 75, p. 76, p. 77, p. 79, p. 81, p. 82, p. 85, p. 88, p. 89, p. 93, p. 97, p. 99, p. 101, p. 103, p. 106, p. 107, p. 108, p. 109, p. 100, p. 112, p. 113, p. 118, p. 199 (bottom), p. 122, p. 123 (top), p. 124, p. 127, p. 130, p. 139, p. 143 to 157.

First published by Hachette-Livre, 43 Quai de Grenelle, Paris 75905, Cedex 15, under the title
Le Grand Guide de l'Encadrement.

This edition published by
Hachette Illustrated UK, Octopus Publishing Group,
2–4 Heron Quays, London E14 4JP

English language translation produced by Translate-A-Book, Oxford
Typesetting by Organ Graphic, Abingdon

ISBN: 1844300137

Printed in Singapore by Tien Wah Press Pte Ltd.